THE ALIEN'S GUIDE TO FRANCE

· JIM WATSON ·

SURVIVAL BOOKS • LONDON • ENGLAND

First published 1999

Survival Books Limited, Suite C, Third Floor
Standbrook House, 2-5 Old Bond Street
London W1X 3TB, United Kingdom
Tel. (44) 171-493 4244, Fax (44) 171-491 0605
E-mail: enquiries@survivalbooks.net
Internet: survivalbooks.net

British Library Cataloguing in Publication Data.
A CIP record for this book is available from the British Library.
ISBN 1 901130 65 7

Printed and bound in Great Britain by Page Bros (Norwich) Ltd.,
Mile Cross Lane, Norwich, Norfolk NR6 6SA, UK.

Contents

France as seen by the rest of the world

The world as seen by France

Introduction

France. Wonderful country. Shame about the French. The rest of the world doesn't understand them.

The French don't even understand themselves. Generations of the country's greatest philosophers have driven themselves to early graves delving and probing into the deepest and darkest nether regions of the French psyche in an ultimately futile search for enlightenment. In their countless volumes of conclusions, all as impenetrable and elusive as the subjects themselves, there has never been one which has conclusively explained the unique love-hate relationship that this most vibrant but unpredictable of people have with the rest of the world. This book is no exception.

However, it can prepare you for the unexpected in a country pulsating with the unexpected. I'm indebted to a rabble of well-established national stereotypes who in the guise of amiable character actors have heroically ignored the tyranny of political correctness to represent in totality the population of France. No mean feat in a country of sixty million rabid individuals. So please be tolerant. Their broad-brush representation of the French character may not tally with yours. Put it down to overacting in search of a cheap laugh.

This guide sets out to conduct you through the main danger areas where you are likely to encounter the unfamiliar French lifestyle. Hopefully, it will equip you with a smattering of knowledge and evasive tactics that will minimise the risk of you being found out, pointed at and labelled that loathsome figure of fun and ridicule in any country: an ignorant foreigner.

Jim Watson

April 1999

Geography

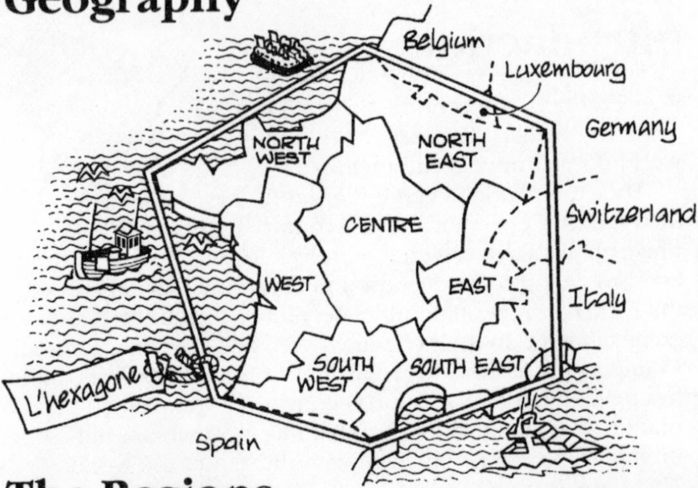

Belgium
Luxembourg
Germany
Switzerland
Italy
Spain

NORTH WEST
NORTH EAST
CENTRE
WEST
EAST
SOUTH WEST
SOUTH EAST

L'hexagone

The Regions

What is it like?

Food

The North West

Brittany: Arthurian legends. Rugged coastline with pretty ports. Inland: forests, stone farmhouses and moorland.
Normandy: Pastoral. Apple orchards, half-timbered farmhouses and contented cows in cosy valleys. Medieval towns and cities.

Soft cheeses, notably Camembert, and other dairy products. Calf's trotters and Rouen duck, killed by choking to avoid bloodshed! Superb fish and seafood. *Crêpes* (v. thin pancakes) filled with seafood, ham cheese, mushrooms, eggs etc. Sweet *crêpes* have chocolate, fruit or jam fillings. Yummy.

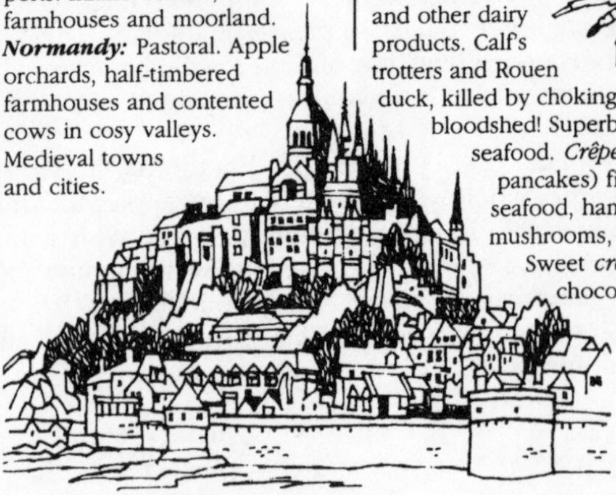

Mont-St-Michel, Normandy

France is the second largest country in Europe, after the reunified Germany, which according to the French (who are experts) cheated its way to the top of the 'Size Does Matter league' by merging its East and West divisions.

The country has six sides, not quite a true hexagon (the classic symbol of order and stability) but close enough for France's sixty million population to consider its shape to be an accurate and appropriate representation of their country's character. They also maintain that France has everything that anybody needs for a happy and fulfilled life. With a rich and varied geography; wonderful food and drink; and people as warm, stimulating and unpredictable as the landscape; it's an opinion that's difficult to disagree with.

The French economy is solidly based on agriculture, with almost 90% of the land productive. The rest is Paris.

Unusually for Europe, France has three distinct climates – continental, marine and sub-tropical. For visitors, it has just two. Hot and cold – love us or leave us.

Drink

Cider: Made from local apples. They are also distilled to make the very potent (at least 40% alcohol!), **Calvados**.
Benedictine: Brandy-based liqueur flavoured with herbs. Those monks know how to make a drink.

The rock formation popularly known as 'the elephant come to drink' on the Normandy coastline

Famous for

Asterix the Gaul: Comic strip accurately depicting Normans as just out of the stone age.
Bayeux Tapestry: Early comic strip celebrating the Norman conquest of England.
D-Day landing sites: Where the English and allied troops landed in 1944 and liberated France. Foolishly, they then gave it back to the French.
Joan of Arc: First Brits-out martyr and French heroine. Burnt at the stake for heresy (at Rouen in 1431) by the fickle French (with British help).
Channel Tunnel: Links Calais with England to make English shopper invasion easier.

The North West

The North East

Le Nord and Picardy: Flat and agricultural. Windmills and pretty canals.

Champagne: Rolling plains, immense forests, deep gorges and vast rivers.

Lorraine: Industrial but with some fine medieval towns and villages. Popular with walkers.

Alsace: Mountains, forests and farmland. Picturesque fortified towns and long ribbons of vineyards winding around pastel-painted villages.

Hearty hot-pots, stews and soups. The famous egg pie (*quiche lorraine*) and pickled cabbage *(sauerkraut)*. Ardennes ham and Andouillettes sausages. Rich cakes and sugar-coated sweetmeats.

Alsace

The East

Franche-Comtè: Tranquil farmland in the Sâone valley, Swiss-style alpine scenery to the east. Mecca for climbers, hikers, and makers of cow bells.

French Alps: Unrivalled mountain scenery. Lakes, dense forests, rivers and gorges. Mega-mecca for outdoor sports and broken leg repairers.

Savoy: Much fought-over Alpine province on the Italian border.

Rhône Valley: (Extends to the south coast) Marshland and rich agriculture in the north. Orchards, sunflowers, lavender, vineyards and olive groves in the south. Mountains, pretty spa towns and deep river gorges in the Ardèche.

Bresse corn-fed chickens and wild fowl. Farmhouse cheeses, fondues and soufflés. Chamonix ham, smoked sausages and fish from glacier-fed lakes.

Savoy traditional dress

Savoy traditional winter dress

Drink	Famous for

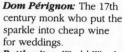

Champagne: 200 million bottles produced a year.

White wines: Cool summers produce Riesling, Gewürztraminer, Muscat, Pinot and Moselle.

Beer: It keeps the German neighbours happy.

Dom Pérignon: The 17th century monk who put the sparkle into cheap wine for weddings.

Battle sites: World War I and II. The Somme.

Strasbourg: HQ of European Union. Where France wins every battle.

Reims Cathedral: French kings crowned here until one lost his head and made it impossible.

Charles de Gaulle: Dour war leader and president who, when he wasn't hiding in London from the Germans, lived and died in Champagne (the non-bubbly variety, of course).

Alsace traditional dress. The Mickey Mouse ears are possibly the first recorded Disney incursion into France

The North East

Rich, red, nose in the glass **Beaujolais** and the superior, nose in the air *cru* wines.

Vin jaune: Yellow wine from the Jura region.

Chartreuse: A herbal liqueur flavoured with saffron, cinnamon and mace. Another liqueur is flavoured with Grenoble walnuts.

Lyon: France's second city and gastronomic capital.

Winter Olympic Games: Albertville 1992 and Grenoble 1968.

Mont Blanc: The highest mountain in Europe to die on (15,770ft).

Smart ski resorts: Teeming with jet-set, beautiful people.

La Marseillaise: Originally a marching song (for locals fleeing from the jet-set) written in this area by Rouget-de-lisle.

The East

Mont Blanc

Languedoc-Roussillon:
Huge variety of scenery and climate, from the sun-baked Mediterranean coastal plain to the cold winters and sparsley populated foothills of the Massif Central. Mainly agricultural, producing half of France's table wine. Roman temples, castle ruins on vast crags and a distinct Spanish influence.

Provence/Côte d'Azur:
Sun, beaches and pretty fishing villages. Plummeting gorges, Carmague salt flats and the most seductive countryside in France, a vast lavender-scented garden of blazing colour.
Cezanne, Van Gogh and Peter Mayle country.

Olive oil with everything. Lots of seafood dishes, fish stews and soups.
Cassoulet, a heavy bean soup cooked with duck or goose.
Paella and Ratatouille.
Provence produces 80% of all French truffles. Frogs legs are also a delicacy. (But what do they do with the rest of the frog?)

Midi-Pyrénées: Rugged coastal and mountainous area of wild, unspoiled beauty separating France from Spain. Stronghold of the hot-blooded Basque people who originated the French beret.

Gascony: Ancient land of the Three Musketeers. Rural with beautiful medieval towns and fortified villages, undulating vineyards and armagnac houses.

Basques enjoy hearty country fare, *poule-au-pot* or *confit ,* salted meat or game cooked and preserved in goose fat. Spanish influenced cuisine – red chilli peppers, vegetables cooked with garlic and salted river fish. Local cheese is red-skinned when made from sheep's milk and black-skinned when made from cow's milk. Thick-skinned Périgord is responsible for *foie gras.*

Drink

Vin de table:
Basic red table wine the French love – rough and immature. That's the wine of course, not the French who as everyone knows are always smooth and mellow.

Pont du Gard,
Languedoc-Roussillon

Armagnac: Grape brandy aged in wooden barrels. Dry white or red **Jurançon wine.**

Rocamadour,
Quercy

Famous for

Monaco: Playground of the rich and infamous. Ruled over by the Grimaldis, France's very own gossip-column Royal Family.
Cannes: Epitome of style, hugely expensive yachts and tasteless film festivals.
Arles: Bullfighting centre where Van Goch misread the script and cut off his own ear instead of the bull's.
French Rugby: Cauliflower ears.
The Mistral: Bitterly cold wind that blows for weeks whenever the French rugby team loses.

Toulouse: High-tech capital of France and home of the high-noise Concorde.
Lourdes: Attracts six million pilgrims a year in search of a miracle cure.
Tour de France: Cyclists racing up mountain passes pursued by drug testers.
Condom: Town that has nothing at all to do with THE condom. Yet sniggering tourists still pack the post office, eager to have its name stamped on their French letters.

The South East

The South West

What is it like?

Food

Loire Valley: The 'garden of France'. Meandering flatlands extending well inland. The grandest of grand châteaux and cathedrals. Sleepy hamlets. Troglodyte caves.

Poitou and Aquitaine: Long Atlantic coastline with sandy beaches, nudists and tourists. Rolling hills, colourful orchards and lazy rivers. Turbulent history. World's largest and most famous vineyards around Bordeaux.

Game, fish, and fresh vegetables. Eels, oysters and mussels along coastline. Salty lamb and goat's cheeses inland. Bayonne ham is world famous. Around Bordeaux, wine is found in practically every dish (and chef).

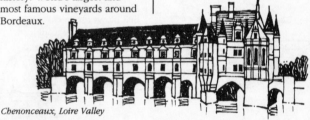

Chenonceaux, Loire Valley

Massif Central: Huge plateau and mountainous area almost one-sixth the area of France. The lush Auverge has extinct volcanoes, deep gorges, green valleys, vast forests, geysers and rivers. Also Romanesque churches, medieval castles and Renaissance palaces. The Limousin is a gentler pastoral paradise of 1,000 lakes.

Burgundy: Rural soul of France. Wealthy vineyards. Historic towns. Romanesque architecture. 750 miles of canals.

Dordogne: Gently rural 'little England'. (According to the English anyway)

Real country fare: *Coq au vin, Boeuf Bourguignon* with Charolais beef. Pork and wild fowl. Fresh water fish. Potatoes, cabbage and wild berries. Dairy products and candied apricots. Burgundy gave the world snails to eat. The world said 'ugh!'

The Auvergne

Drink	Famous for

The West

Drink

Wine: Awash with it. Huge variety. From aged Château Mouton-Rothschild reds to elegant, sweet Sauternes and crisp white Bordeaux.

Cognac: The world's most expensive brandy, distilled from the local most expensive wine.

Cointreau: The famous liqueur of Anjou, flavoured on the cheap with orange peel.

Famous for

Wine Châteaux: Bordeaux has over 10,000, some little more than a vine, a press and a bottle.

Castles: In the 12th and 13th centuries Aquitaine was part of England and Bordeaux was the fourth largest 'English' city. Poor grape harvests are still blamed on the English.

The Loire: France's longest river – 628 miles. But not as long (or as deep) as the EU wine river.

Le Mans 24 hours motor race: In the rest of France they race all the time.

The Centre

Wine: Hugely venerated and expensive Côte d'Or. Sweet Burgundy, light and fruity Beaujolais, dry white Chablis and various Chardonnays.

Mineral water: From the cold springs of Perrier and Vichy.

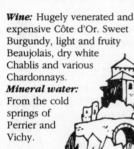

French presidents even more dour than de Gaulle: Pompidou and Giscard d'Estaing were both Auvergnats.

The undour Michelin Man: and restaurant star benefactor.

Vichy: Seat of the infamous wartime puppet government.

Chapelle St-Michel d'Alguilhe, The Auvergne

Paris

The Paris area has 20% of the country's population, 90% of its foreign tourists and 100% of the most aggressive drivers in the world. Apart from people and traffic, it is also packed with the essence of all France, concentrated and magnified to extremes. What is good is very good. What is bad is awful.

The Seine: River which divides the city in two. Often hidden from view by huge floating greenhouses packed with tourists.

Left Bank: South of the Seine. Haunt of artists, intellectuals and revolutionaries.

Right Bank: North of the Seine. Grand, glamourous and chic. The banker's bank.

Pompidou Centre: Avant-garde collection of pipes, ducts and cables housing a museum and a gallery of modern art. Paris's top tourist attraction. Constantly being repaired.

Latin quarter: Students, artists, book shops, galleries, cafés and political unrest.

Opera Quarter: Busy commerce, tourism and shopping centre by day; lively club and theatre land by night. It has been said that if you sit here long enough the whole world will pass you by. You have to get a seat first though.

Eiffel Tower: A temporary structure for the 1889 Universal Exhibition, the tower still stands, a massive symbol of French potency.

Dôme Church: Resting place of Napoleon, encased in six coffins, one inside the other. It makes him look taller.

Pavement cafés: Traditional meeting places to relax and watch the world go by. But beware, a wide footpath can also become a convenient overtaking lane for hard-pressed motorists. And in Paris, that's all of them.

The Louvre: Houses one of the world's greatest art collections, including the *Mona Lisa*. Provokes English lavatorial jokes, but that's not why she's smiling.

Arc de Triomphe: Celebrates Napoleon's victories. Twelve broad and straight boulevards radiating from the arch give Paris its modern and airy look, but they were also designed to give a clear shot for the artillery in case of revolt.

Montmartre: Artists-artists, tourists-tourists and can-can.

Notre-Dame: Stunning Gothic architecture – rose windows, flying buttresses and gargoyles – but no Quasimodo.

Another part of France...

Corsica:
Barren rocky island in the Mediterranean, 100 miles off the French south coast. Best known for mindless political terrorism carried out in the name of independence and as the birthplace of the short (in stature) dictator: Napoleon Bonaparte, Emperor of France between 1804-14.

History

40,000 BC: The first French artist paints pictures of animals on cave walls. Soon after, the first art critic arrives.

1000BC: A Celtic tribe of Gauls settle and names the country after themselves.

52BC: The Romans conquer the Gauls and spread their influence throughout the land. Roads are built and chariot jams block the main route to the south.

AD486: A Germanic tribe, the Franks, drive out the Romans and rename the country France.

AD800: Charlemagne, King of the Franks, conquers Europe and sets a French precedent for all time.

AD845: Norsemen, also known as Normans or Vikings, settle in what they name Normandy. 'Vikingdy' didn't sound right.

1066: The Normans invade Britain, defeat the English King Harold at Hastings and their leader is crowned William the Conqueror. He stars in an early soap opera, The Bayeux Tapestry.

The next 500 years: The Middle Ages. France is rocked by midlife crisis. The rulers of different parts of the country battle to find a single national leader thus founding the modern French political system.

1337 to 1453: France fights The Hundred Years' War with England to establish how many years there are in a hundred.

1643: King Louis XIV, declares himself the 'Sun King' and becomes a role model for Frenchmen ever since. He builds himself a huge theme park near Paris, at Versailles.

1789: The French poor take to the streets in violent revolution to demand their own theme park. King Louis XVI and Queen Marie-Antoinette are guillotined and the First Republic is established. Throughout the country 17,000 others are also beheaded. By 1794, the revolutionists run out of victims and execute their own leaders.

1799: A Corsican general, Napoleon Bonaparte, becomes the people's leader. He conquers much of Europe and shows king-like tendencies by crowning himself Emperor. In an invasion too far, he is beaten by the Russian winter and is exiled to the island of Elba.

1815: The monarchy is restored. Napoleon escapes from Elba, raises an army and resumes his European campaign. He loses The Big Match against the English at Waterloo and is exiled to the island of Saint Helena, where he dies in 1821.

1848: The people rise up again, the monarchy is got rid of (again) and the Second Republic begins under Napoleon's useless nephew, Louis. He tries his hand at the family business of Empire building, does badly in the Crimean War, then is defeated and taken prisoner when he invades Prussia. The people revolt again and the Third Republic is declared as the Prussians advance on Paris.

History

1939: France and Britain declare war on Germany when Chancellor Adolf Hitler invades Poland.

1940: France capitulates after German armoured divisions avoid the Maginot Line (a supposedly impregnable wall of fortifications along the Franco-German border) by simply going round it through Belgium. The Germans occupy the north and west of the country and set up a puppet government at Vichy in the south led by an aging WW1 hero, General Pétain.

1871: The monarchists are reinstated. After they surrender the provinces of Alsace and Lorraine to the German occupiers the people take to the streets. Over 20,000 Communard rebels are executed.

1914: Germany declares war on Russia and France at start of First World War. France regains Alsace and Lorraine but 1.3 million Frenchmen are killed and another million crippled. Trench warfare devastates much of north-eastern France and the country faces financial crisis.

1919: The Treaty of Versailles ends the war and Germany pays France huge reparations.

1944: British, US and Canadian troops liberate France. General de Gaulle, who boldly led the French Resistance movement from the safety of London, returns in triumph and sets up a provisional government.

1946: De Gaulle resigns, calculating that the people will demand his return. Forever fickle, they do not. Instead they vote for a new constitution, the Fourth Republic, and yet another period of political unrest.

1958: Extreme right-wingers threaten a military coup and possible civil war over the government's 'defeatist' attitude to Algerian independence. De Gaulle is brought back as peacemaker and sets up the Fifth Republic.

1961: Britain applies to join the EEC. De Gaulle says 'Non'.

1962: De Gaulle ends the war in Algeria and 750,000 Algerian-French citizens pour into France to join others from similar liberated French colonies and protectorates in Africa. The economy is stretched, unemployment rises and racial tension grows.

1967: Britain again tries to join the EEC. Again De Gaulle says 'Non'.

1968: Workers join a Paris student demonstration sparking a general strike of nine million people. Widespread reforms halt a new revolution.

1970: De Gaulle dies.

1973: Britain joins the EEC.

To present: France, now closely allied with its old enemy, Germany, gradually takes control of Europe through their dominance of the European Union.

National Identity

The French care deeply about what matters in life – being French. They are convinced, despite evidence to the contrary, that in corporate, moral and individual matters they are superior to the rest of the universe and beyond. To the French there is only one correct way to do anything – the French way.

Hardly surprising then that the rest of the world sees them as arrogant and self-obsessed. Typically, the French do not consider arrogance and self-obsession to be negative. To them they are qualities to be admired. After all, arrogance and self-obsession are French inventions, so to the French they can only be virtues.

The French see brilliance in everything they do. Louis XIV was dubbed the Sun King and despite having got rid of their Royals (in the spirit of true revolution the people now consider themselves all to be kings or queens) his omnipotent aura still shines brightly across the country.

French people are deeply patriotic, and moved to tears by the symbol of the republic, the romantic image of Marianne, a

young, bare-breasted peasant woman, musket in hand, leaping the barricades of the glorious revolution. Modern French banknotes and stamps display her likeness, which bears a striking resemblance to the actress, Catherine Deneuve.

Despite their insularity, however, the French do acknowledge that the rest of the world exists, but only as a bench mark for their own superiority. The more inferior the rest of the world appears,

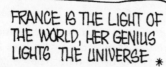

FRANCE IS THE LIGHT OF THE WORLD, HER GENIUS LIGHTS THE UNIVERSE *

the more superior France becomes in comparison.

It helps if you humiliate the rest of the world. The Belgians and Swiss are the butt of French jokes for their refined French accents and cultural heritage. America is abhorred for their contamination of the French young with fast food, rap music and Euro Disney. Britain is hated for... well, just being Britain.

● Wrapping yourself in the French flag may help you to be accepted, but beware! The French may despise the rest of the world, but they reserve their greatest emnity for their fellow citizens. Even the Parisians hate Parisians! Always remember that the French are Basques, Bretons, Normans, or whatever first and French a distant second.

* Of course de Gaulle said it in French. A French patriot to die for, (many did) he was never heard to utter a word of English, even when he was actually speaking French. His accent was so bad his audience thought he was still speaking French.

CHARLES de GAULLE

LEADER OF FRENCH RESISTANCE DURING WORLD WAR II

PRESIDENT OF FRANCE 1958-1969 & NOW AN AIRPORT

The French 21

Character

The French are attracted to all things vibrant, alive, and emotional; a public, unembarrassed people who love to talk and argue about ideas and being up to date. They enjoy ideals, concepts, innovations and tinkering about with things, like monarchy, nuclear weapons, and the European Union.

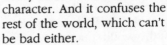

France is a land of sixty million philosophers, all of them constantly discussing at length the latest in everything and anything. Talk is cheap in France and the French buy lots of it. But for them the latest fad never lasts long and they quickly pass on to the next talking point. Not for nothing is *passé* a French concept.

The Big Idea in France is the Big Idea itself. It's not the end product that's important, it's the getting there that is everything. What is finally produced may be a disaster, but the concept was a triumph.

The rest of the world interprets this attitude as typical French inconsistency; saying one thing and doing another. The French, typically, see inconsistency as a consistent strength, woven like DNA into every thread of French character. And it confuses the rest of the world, which can't be bad either.

● Whatever you do in France do it with style and panache. Above all, don't give a thought about what anyone else thinks. The French will denounce you in public but secretly admire the way you did it. And you can't get more French than that.

Values

Despite their apparent *laissez-faire* attitude to life the French are sticklers for codes of conduct. In what they consider to be the perfect society (France), the foundations – diplomacy, art, ethics, fashion, literature and the law – must be done in the right way, in the right place and at the right time.

Tradition rules above all. The French like revolution, pulling things to bits and starting again, but usually end up with something much the same.

Petty regulations – that is those the French disagree with, usually concerned with driving, parking, smoking or hygiene – are routinely ignored.

Sitting on the fence has no place in France. You must always have an opinion about everything. Your opinion will probably be ignored but it will always be valued. If you do not express an opinion, an undertaker will be summoned to measure you up.

It's also important to be serious about things that matter and to be capable of discussing them with anyone. The entire country allegedly read the Maastrict Treaty in 1992 before voting in the referendum on EU membership. The claim was never questioned by the rest of the world as a) no one else knew what the treaty was about – even the writers, and b) no one else was interested anyway.

● Regard rules as only mild suggestions but observe formalities as if they carry the death penalty. Remember this is the country that showed the world how to fight a duel at dawn with rapiers and how to lose your head with style on the guillotine.

Roots

The French have a passion for roots. They like the security, the reliability and the feeling that their feet are forever stuck in the soil. Beneath the nails of every Parisian office worker there ferments the metaphorical dregs of the French countryside, lodged there from countless years of tilling the blessed earth. The image of the burly farmer, swilling rough cider, forcing grain down tethered geese for *foie gras* and blasting animals to oblivion is one that is dear to all French people.

The ownership of land arouses huge passions. France is a big country but every French person wants more than their fair share. Family squabbles and feuds over land are commonplace. The ownership of a soggy ditch or a patch of nettles can result in centuries of infighting. However, the French are quite happy to sell land to any foreigner who will pay a hyper-inflated price for it. Going to war with your relatives to secure a few grains of soil is well worth the sacrifice if you can easily sell them later to a gullible foreigner. The French love of the land empowers the rural community with outrageous political clout. Farmers are notoriously quick to take action against authority, dumping vegetables outside town halls and herding cattle along elegant Parisian boulevards at the slightest provocation. As action against authority is a quality revered in France as much as the love of the land itself, the status of the modern French farmer is that of national folk hero.

Class

Despite the ghastly shadow cast across it by Madame Guillotine, the French class system continues to wield a significant if more subtle influence on the country.

The Grande Bourgeoisie: The upper class. Barons and Counts. Old families whose names have graced French society for centuries. Rarely speak to or even notice anyone outside their own class. They only look down. But do relate to the peasants, who also know their place.

The Bonne Bourgeoisie: The flashy, new-money class. High-profile sports stars, fashion designers and artists. They look forward rather than back, convinced that they are the future of France. Will speak to anyone. Least complaining, except about taxes.

The Petite Bourgeoisie look up to the upper class but look down on the *Bonne Bourgeoisie* whom they consider to be vulgar working class with too much money. They complain most, especially about how little taxes the *Bonne Bourgeoisie* pay.

The Peasants know their place and look up to nobody. They also know that everyone else would like to be them anyway.

Social Customs

Beneath the relaxed veneer of French everyday life lies a backbone of formality, stiffened and eager to trip up the unwary newcomer. The man who combs his hair in public. The women who applies her make-up or takes off her jacket as she walks along a sunny street. Indeed, anyone who addresses someone they have just met by their first name. All of them are guilty of a serious social gaffe. A *faux pas* no less. The French, as usual, always have a phrase for it.

In social slip-ups the language has a lot to answer for. Take just two words: *tu* and *vous*. Their use depends on how well you know the person you're talking to. The difficulty is how to gauge **when** you know the person you're talking to well enough. It's simplest to wait until the other person lets you know, probably by accusing you of being stand-offish!

So let's be clear. Always address strangers as *vous*. The familiar *tu* can be safely used in the presence of God, children or a dog, but use it with the dog's owner and you may end up with the dog (your friend) being set on you. Simple. Less easy to ascertain is where the Social Customs Police stand when Frenchmen are relieving themselves. Well out of the way usually. Frenchmen pee all over the place. On the side of the road. Facing the traffic. While they're smoking or reading a newspaper or eating a pie. Remember, never address an unknown Frenchman in full flood as *tu*. He'd be disgusted.

If you're introduced to a French person you should say good day in French (*bonjour*), add their title (*madame, monsieur* or *whatever*) and shake hands in French (that's one pump only, no bone crushing, and definitely no secret signs). When you say goodbye (*au revoir*) you shake hands again. With everyone in the room.

Go into a shop and the proprietor will expect you to say good day or good evening with the appropriate title. *Bonjour* becomes *bonsoir* around 1800 or after dark. Problems can arise if the skies darken during a thunderstorm at 1500. When you leave, say goodbye (*au revoir*) and the title. Do not say good night (*bonne nuit*) even if it is night. You only say *bonne nuit* when you're going to bed.

Which brings us to kissing, the biggest social minefield an alien in France will ever have to negotiate. Get it wrong and there can be red faces all round. Men don't kiss unless they are intimate friends or have just had a medal pinned on them by the President. Take your cue from the French. If a women wants you to kiss her she will offer her cheek. The kiss itself must be only a light brush of the upper cheek. Keep your feelings under control and your tongue firmly in **your** cheek.

The number of kisses increases as you move south. In the north, one kiss on each cheek is sufficient. In St Tropez the number becomes almost obscene.

● You may decide at this point that it would be simpler not to risk any contact at all with French people and just enjoy their country instead. The French people won't mind. They'll just think you're an ignorant foreigner. As they would have done anyway.

Men, Women and Families

A Frenchman sees himself as an irresistible cocktail of flamboyant sportsman and passionate poet; someone who knows all there is to know about women and can play them like a violin.

In reality, he's usually shorter than Frenchmen appear in films. He's a family man who plays boules (bowls with smaller balls). He wouldn't recognise a line of poetry unless it referred to cyclists in the Tour de France and would only play Aviolin if he could score goals for Marseille.

He drinks and smokes too much, washes too little and falls asleep too easily in female company. He loves his country to the point of xenophobia and his eyes mist over at the crow of the cockerel – the symbol of France.

The cockerel is a colourful bird which makes a lot of noise, chases away strangers, copulates frequently, has to produce no eggs, and ends up cooked in wine. Most Frenchmen ask for nothing more.

Surprisingly for a country that treats most living things in a callous and often cruel manner, the affection lavished on French cats and dogs approaches the divine. But, as any gourmet will testify, before it can attain truly divine status an animal must first be eaten.

French children look like angels and behave like devils. They are loved, cossetted and encouraged to speak out at an early age. Once they start talking they never stop. Anarchy breaks out as soon as they are let off the lead. Usually when they are on a school trip abroad. French children, like French mime artists, do not travel well.

The popular image of French women as elegant, intelligent and good in bed is one that French women work hard at to make it look easy and natural. French women wield their power over men with a subtle but devastating mix of femininity and feminism – available but strictly on her terms. This man-killing appeal is not restricted to just the city chic. The image of a rosy-cheeked earth mother carrying a basket of bread and wine along a country lane is equally seductive to the rural *roué*, wherever he may come from. The universal fatal attraction of French women is that they know men do not know everything there is to know about them, but are clever enough to allow men to think they do.

The elderly French aren't dumped into residential homes. They are cared for at home, where they continue to be a respected part of the extended family, not just as cheap babysitters or cooks but with an equal say in everything. They are always included in family plans, even joining the younger members on holiday.

Though the institution of marriage is on the decline and a third end in divorce, French couples still set up homes together and build the conventional nuclear family unit.

Private life in France is kept private. Dalliances by either partner has little effect on their public or professional life. Unless that is, either of them is a politician, when a public, over-active sex life is a guaranteed vote catcher.

Religion

France is traditionally Catholic but only because England isn't. The eleventh commandment in France states thou shalt not do anything like the English. The French also like the notion that it's okay to sin as long as you repent afterwards.

Religion is no longer a big issue in France. Church attendance has slumped to 10 per cent in some cities and the great cathedrals have been largely taken over by mammon. Sponsors logos adorn the high altars and devoted priests relieve tourists of the great earthly burden of money, which they redirect to the glory of Socialist revolution in remote South American rain forests.

The French may have abandoned many of the duties and burdens of religion but cunningly kept all the feast days, saints' days, France is Blessed days, God We Won the World Cup! days, 365 We Hate the Rest of the World days and the just plain and simple days off. France has more holidays than any other nation in the world. Yet another example of the French picking out the good things in life, abandoning the rest and having no conscience at all as to the consequence.

● For a 'miracle cure' join the queues of hopeful pilgrims at France's most important religious shrine, Our Lady of Lourdes. The British Conservative party and French communists are regular visitors.

Sex

Sex permeates ever facet of French life. It sells everything from cars to mineral water. The nipple count in prime time television adverts would trigger a station close down in less liberated countries.

The French boast that they invented condoms, adultery, sadism, brothels, and even masturbation. And, as they regard their country as the original Garden of Eden, the sex act itself.

Flirting, like most things French, is an art form where sexual overtones are an acceptable part and parcel of every-day life. The French have mobile and expressive faces and a seductive language with separated nouns which creates a masculine and feminine tension in every sentence. Even the pronunciation of many words requires the mouth to pucker up into a kissable pout.

French women lose their virginity at the age of 18 (official figures). Frenchmen lose it at the age of nine (Frenchmen's figures). But the Frenchman as great lover may be a myth. All mouth and no trousers. Many French women complain of unsatisfactory sex lives and *c'est normal* for them to take lovers to make up the shortfall.

● Despite one in ten Frenchmen having an impotence problem, when a factory to manufacture the virility drug, Viagra, opened in the Loire Valley, French manhood was so insulted an official spokesman had to assure the world that the drug was for export only.

Health

Given their eating and drinking habits, it's hardly surprising that the French view every ailment as being due to malfunction of their livers. The cure is to drink gallons of mineral water to flush out the organ. Failing that the entire system has to be purged, which means turning to the French cure-all: the suppository.

> BUT ENOUGH ABOUT MY LIVER, HOW IS YOURS?

France is a nation of hypochondriacs, all finely tuned to every creak of their bodies. Hence France has a lot of doctors. Sadly, not always in rural areas (unless there's a handy golf course). Here treatment is down to a wise old member of the family, who usually prescribes suppositories.

> THE MEDICINE
> First, lower your trousers...

French people are not registered with one doctor, so they cart their medical records around with them to read at their leisure. The average French patient knows more about his or her medical history than any doctor ever could. Armed with that information they will argue their case with any medical person or indeed with anyone who will listen.

Unless seriously ill, a French person will go to a pharmacist rather than a doctor. The pharmacist listens to the patient's self-diagnosis and then suggests a pill or a potion. The workings of the medicine is recorded in great detail on the box top. Including where to insert it.

Personal Hygiene

When Emperor Napoleon Bonaparte dispatched his message from the battlefield to Josephine: 'Home in a month. Stop washing now', he set a standard for French personal hygiene that has changed little since. In France, natural body odours are a powerful aphrodisiac. To wash them away is to deny an elementary force of nature. BO is OK. A French family of four uses only one bar of soap a month. And that's the month they have all their relatives to stay.

Body smells may mean sex to the French, but they also mean money. Lots of it. The French are the world's leading perfumers, happy to sell tiny phials of liquid to the rest of the planet for exorbitant prices to mask the smells that they themselves find so seductive.

The bidet is another example of French inventiveness and remarkable ability to exploit a marketing opportunity. Regarded throughout the rest of the world as a highly sophisticated answer to the ticklish problem of washing one's private parts, the bidet was actually designed as a made to measure toilet by a diminutive Frenchman peed off at having to stand on a box to relieve himself at a toilet of conventional height.

● If you intend to stay for some time in France, adopt the French system of personal hygiene. Take a regular bath. On your birthday. Whether you need to or not.

Language

French is the language of love, food and the gods. In France it enjoys divine status, with a number of august bodies dedicated to keeping it free of any foreign adulterations and defilement.

If you want to enjoy the rich patois of French life you need an intimate knowledge of their beautiful and subtle language. However, an ability to speak the language does not necessarily guarantee that you will understand the French (or that they will understand you).

So rather than waste years learning 'correct' French, you can take the easy route and just use *merde!* (the most used expletive) and *Non!* (the most used word). Coupled with expansive body language, these two easily-remembered words can effectively deal with any situation. Generally the French say no to everything and only afterwards consider the question. De Gaulle based his long political career on his ability to say *NON!*

Many French people pretend not to speak English, often because they speak it badly and do not wish to appear foolish in front of foreigners. However, French youth increasingly speaks perfect English. To the older generation this merely confirms the country's cultural decline.

● When conversing in French, butt in at all times whether you've got anything significant to say or not. The French consider it proves that you're listening.

Body Language

As all foreigners know, the best way to communicate with the natives is to shout at them in English at close quarters. If this does not work or you are sensitive about personal safety, you should stick to finger-pointing, smiling and general sublimation. Those of a more adventurous nature may like to try some of the subtle French arts of gesture, signing and mime.

'I do not need a drink.' 'I need a drink.'

Le bras d'honneur: The supreme gesture. At its mildest it means 'up yours' but used with passion it can mean something much stronger:

1. Stretch out your right arm in front of you.

2. Smack your right bicep with your left hand. At the same time...

3. Snap your right forearm smartly upwards.

Warning!
It is not advisable to make this gesture in the general direction of a gendarme, anyone with a gun, or indeed anyone bigger than yourself.

The Look:
The most subtle of French body language. Use with care. It can mean different things to different people.

The Classic French Shrug: A massive cultural icon. Basically an elaborate mime, it is more usually delivered with an emphatic vocal accompaniment:

1. ERR... **2.** ERRRRR... **3.** NON!

Rolling eyes
Spit   Pout
Refinements

Warning! Do not attempt to mimic this gesture. The French would consider it a huge insult. Of course, if that's what you intend...

Insults

The French are rude to perfection, especially in Paris. There's nothing casual or unthinking about it either. They really mean it.

They are especially rude to strangers. Ring a wrong number on the telephone and you can expect a torrent of abuse from whoever answers, even if it's an answerphone. Friends are routinely rude to each other. It's a measure of the strength of the relationship. Rude one day, forgotten the next.

Waiters serve rudeness with all the aplomb they give to the food. Generally, the greater the waiter's disdain the better the quality of the food.

City taxi drivers are masters of the shrugged expletive and the exasperated eye-roll. They have volatility written into

their CVs and can be impressively rude even with their backs to you.

Rudeness is not restricted to French males. Complain about the fit of a dress and the female shop assistant will inevitably blame it on Madame's *immense* size.

However, what seems like hostility to the visitor is simply a national sport to the French, rather like a more vigorous game of *boules*. The only hope for visitors is to learn the rules and join in.

● Always keep your cool or you'll lose face. Only go ballistic if it's really necessary – such as in disagreements over driving, food, drink or sport. Above all, bear in mind that any sign of weakness will be ruthlessly exploited and in France the customer is always wrong.

Sensitive Areas

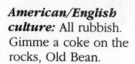

The French view:

Don't mention:

American/English culture: All rubbish. Gimme a coke on the rocks, Old Bean.

American/English language. Fast food. Euro Disney. Modern music. Greenpeace. Animal rights. Nuclear bomb tests.

Sex scandals: Our public figures don't have them.

Public figures are protected by privacy law so French people don't know what they're up to.

The English: Losers. Especially in battles with us. That Wellington couldn't win a Welly Wanging contest.

The English, especially if you're English.

Race problems: Okay we don't win the Tour de France every year but it's still the greatest cycle race in the world.

Xenophobia, immigrants, racial and religious minorities, Basque separatists, Corsica, right wing politicians; the French can ignore anything.

The Common Agricultural Policy: Loads of EU money for French farmers. It must be good.

Butter, beef and cereal mountains. World famine. Setaside. Subsidies. Handouts. Fraud. Hypocrisy. Margaret Thatcher.

The 1998 World Cup: We won and the glory of France burned bright in every corner of the globe.

WE'RE WORLD BEST AT EVERY-THING CUP

Huge home advantage. Familiar venues. Match tickets only sold to French supporters. Biased referees. Final won against a team who refused to play. Star players not born in France.

Eating

Eating is as dear to the French heart as it is to the French stomach, a sensuous, spiritual experience to dissect, discuss and declaim on long after the food has been digested. Some people (not the French) maintain that the French prefer eating to sex. Others (definitely not the French) would say that they're better at eating than sex. Without doubt they do a lot of it. Eating that is.

Few other nations are as devoted to their food as the French and they are among the world's biggest eaters. They will eat anything that walks, crawls, slithers, jumps, swims or flies. No living creature is safe from the French dinner plate. Particular favourites are horsemeat and songbirds, usually eaten raw with lashings of garlic.

Nothing remotely edible goes to waste. Body parts that are normally thrown away by more squeamish eaters are in France elevated to gastronomic delicacies. Hoofs, ears, tails, brains, entrails and reproductive organs are all served up with little attempt to disguise their original identity. Indeed, knowledge of where they came from is considered to add extra spice to their eating.

With such an uninhibited approach to food it's not surprising that the French regard vegetarians with deep suspicion. Anyone who doesn't eat meat is regarded as very strange. Vegans – who don't eat fish or shellfish either – risk having a riot on their pale, anaemic hands when they dine out in a restaurant. Vampires are of course thought quite normal in blood-loving France. Especially when served in a red wine sauce.

Restaurants often display  *their menu on a chalk-written blackboard. You may wish to study it carefully and avoid certain items.*

● To become accepted in France you should be seen to eat at least some of the items from Le Ugh! menu. There's no need to go right through the card at one sitting. That would be considered excessive. Even for a French gourmet.

LE UGH! MENU

Cuisses de grenouilles ~ FROGS LEGS
Escargots ~ SNAILS
Aile ~ BIRD'S WINGS
Anguillette ~ BABY EELS
Cervelle ~ BRAIN
Gras double ~ TRIPE
Mou ~ LUNG
Hure ~ BOAR'S HEAD
Ris ~ PANCREAS
Fraise de veau ~ CALF'S INNARDS
Rognon ~ KIDNEY
Foie ~ LIVER
Fromage de porc ~ PIG'S HEAD
Tête de veau ~ CALF'S HEAD
Rognons blancs/animelles ~ TESTICLES
Cheval ~ HORSE MEAT
Pieds de porc ~ PIG'S TROTTERS
Oreilles de porc ~ PIG'S EARS
Queue de porc ~ PIG'S TAIL
Merles ~ BLACKBIRDS
Ortolans ~ BUNTINGS
Beguinettes ~ WARBLERS
à l'ail ~ WITH GARLIC

BON APPÉTIT!

Eating Out

As befits a nation dedicated to both the worship of food and the worship of itself, France boasts a range of eating places unrivalled anywhere in the universe. Whatever your taste, pocket or waistline you will be well catered for. Just don't ask for foreign (non-French) food.

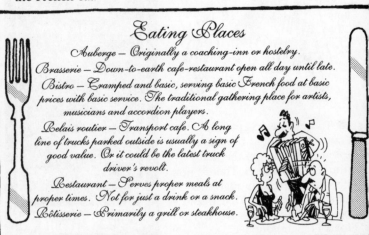

You can pay as much or as little as you like. Foreigners are often amazed at how French restaurants can serve such excellent food at such modest prices. Don't ask. Assume it is just part of the magic of France. That's what the French do.

They also know where to eat well. If you want value for money and can cope with an ambient mix of garlic and *Gauloises*, ignore the plastic tourist troughs and eat where the French eat.

Eating Places

Auberge — Originally a coaching-inn or hostelry.

Brasserie — Down-to-earth cafe-restaurant open all day until late.

Bistro — Cramped and basic, serving basic French food at basic prices with basic service. The traditional gathering place for artists, musicians and accordion players.

Relais routier — Transport cafe. A long line of trucks parked outside is usually a sign of good value. Or it could be the latest truck driver's revolt.

Restaurant — Serves proper meals at proper times. Not for just a drink or a snack.

Rôtisserie — Primarily a grill or steakhouse.

Fixed price menus must be displayed outside restaurants, so you always know what to expect inside. A handwritten menu indicates that either the dishes are changed often or that the owner is too mean to pay a printer. To avoid tourist menus, check the restaurant car park for foreign number plates. Generally, the shorter the menu the better the food. Children are usually welcome – until they ask for beefburgers.

Most restaurants close on Sundays. Some in the country close for lunch! Top class Paris restaurants shut down for all of August to avoid the hordes of plebeian tourists.

Though required by law to provide non-smoking areas, most eating places either ignore the law or offer non-smokers a table where no smoker would ever want to smoke anyway.

Foreign restaurants are difficult to find outside the big cities. An English restaurant opening in France would be regarded by the French as a laughable business venture and the food rated somewhere below pig-swill or American takeaway standard.

● Waiters or waitresses should be addressed as *Monsieur, Madame* or *Mademoiselle*. Never call out *'Garçon'*, snap your fingers or stand up and approach the service person. To do so may seriously effect the standard of service you receive.

Food

Eating in France is pure, unabashed, salivating pleasure. But behind the scenes the preparation of food follows a serious, neo-religious ritual. Master chefs have elevated the simple act of cooking to a high art form, building temples of gastronomy dedicated to the infinitely demanding task of tickling the taste buds of their ever open-mouthed disciples: French gourmets.

Not only masters of cuisine, the chefs have also pulled off the trick of categorising their cooking so even palate-dead foreigners can more easily absorb its subtle delicacies:

Haute cuisine: The cream of French cooking and the most expensive. Consists of a huge repertoire of rich and elaborate sauces made with butter, cream and wine. The variety of exotic ingredients, such as truffles, were originally added to disguise the poor quality of the main ingredients.

Nouvelle cuisine: A healthier version of *haute cuisine* with the emphasis on freshness, lightness and presentation. The tiny helpings of pretty food artily

arranged on large plates often look literally too good to eat. The minimalist concept carries through to minimum cooking to retain natural flavours and sauces designed to enhance rather than hide the taste of the main ingredients.

Cuisine régionale: Cooking indigenous to the different regions of France. Each has its own style and specialities, often influenced by the neighbouring countries.

Cuisine bourgeoise: Plain but excellent fare such as meat or game stews and casseroles made with wine, mushrooms and onions. Very popular, particularly with big eaters.

Cuisine minceur: Gourmet food for slimmers. Similar to *nouvelle cuisine* but without fat, sugar and carbohydrates. Uses fat-free ingredients and tastes of nothing.

While some gourmet foods are highly valued in France they are not necessarily all that special.

The truffle: 'The black winter diamond' to its devotees – is actually a smelly, mis-shapen fungus dug out of the ground by a sex-crazed pig.

Foie gras: The distended liver of ducks and geese force-fed maize through a funnel with an 18 inch spout stuck down their throats to avoid the natural gagging system. The *gavage* takes place four times a day for the last 12 days of the bird's three-month life. Livers grow so much that they almost fill the body cavity, forcing aside lungs, heart and other organs. After the *gavage* a goose liver can weigh up to a kilogram. The livers are sliced up, potted, boiled for 90 minutes then sold at £20 for a small jar.

Despite the rest of the world increasingly grazing on snacks throughout the day, the habit has yet to catch on in France. Meals are still taken at conventional times but they may have different emphasis.

Breakfast: Not important. Often just strong coffee, freshly brewed and served in large bowls. When eaten, breakfast is usually the continental variety – croissants, butter and jam.

Lunch: Most important meal of the day. Sunday lunch is the family highlight of the week and often lasts for most of the day.

Dinner: Served 1900 to 2200. Lighter than lunch though no snack – to be grazed or otherwise.

More Food

Course Etiquette

First Course: *Starter or hors-d'oeuvre – Soup or in classy places a big range of tasty concoctions.*
Second course: *Entrée – Usually only in medium or top class restaurants. Often fish but can be an omelette, chicken, rabbit, frogs' legs or snails.*
Main course: *Traditionally meat though you can choose fish with french fries and common vegetables such as carrots, peas or green beans.*
Cheese Course: *Served after the main course. Always preceeds the dessert.*
A green salad may be served after the main meal.
Dessert: *Undistinguished in humble establishments – ice cream, sorbets, caramel cream, peach melba or fruit. In first class places, as elaborate as the rest of the menu. Strong black coffee in tiny cups, possibly with petit-fours, and brandy or liqueurs.*

All restaurants serve unlimited amounts of delicious bread. Break it with your hands. Don't cut it with a knife. In cheaper places it's common to use the same knife and fork throughout the meal.

bleu
very rare

saignant
rare

à point
medium

bien cuit
well done

For the English and others who prefer their meat cremated there is a further degree:

Bien bien cuit (BBC)

Wine is usually drunk throughout the meal. If you prefer water, order a bottled variety. Tap water has to be provided free but it may never arrive. Bottled water goes on your bill so it will be served with a flourish.

Don't ask for a doggy bag or take your own wine.

OF COURSE THERE'S A FLY IN IT, SIR, ITS FLY SOUP

● The composition and number of courses can vary greatly and there are often surprises. Don't complain too loudly about a snail in your salad – it might be the chef's latest signature dish.

Drinking

The French are convinced that intelligence, sexual prowess and driving skills are all greatly enhanced by a stiff drink or three. With over 15 litres of pure alcohol drunk per splitting head per year, they are the world's most prolific consumers of alcohol. Few get through the day without a tipple.

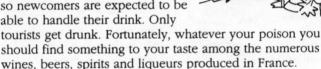

However, French people are rarely seen in a legless condition, so newcomers are expected to be able to handle their drink. Only tourists get drunk. Fortunately, whatever your poison you should find something to your taste among the numerous wines, beers, spirits and liqueurs produced in France.

Wine is the most common drink although export lager beer is also popular, especially with visiting football hooligans who find the empty 25cl bottles perfect missiles. Local cider is drunk in the north and Gin Fizz is oddly popular in the south. The wealthy like to drink whisky, especially malt, which they consider more stylish.

Water from the tap is not hugely popular in France for drinking (or washing). The French prefer something out of a bottle even though mineral water and soft drinks are often dearer than wine or beer.

CHATEAU LAFITTE...
CHATEAU LAFITTE...

● The legal age for drinking in France is 16, though there's virtually no enforcement and children are readily served and sold alcohol everywhere. By the age of 16 they're well used to it anyway. French babies are often weaned on wine mixed with water.

Wine

Like food, sex and religion (it is closely associated with them all), wine is shrouded in mystique. No other drink has such strict laws governing its production or so much pretentious claptrap accompanying its consumption.

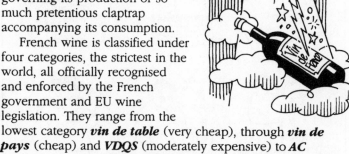

French wine is classified under four categories, the strictest in the world, all officially recognised and enforced by the French government and EU wine legislation. They range from the lowest category *vin de table* (very cheap), through *vin de pays* (cheap) and *VDQS* (moderately expensive) to *AC* (expensive), the highest and most pompous catagory which is applied to around 37% of French output.

In areas such as Bordeaux and Burgundy, where there's a concentration of top producers, wines from top-ranking vineyards are further categorized into growths such as *grand cru* and *premier cru*, denoting the highest quality and astronomically expensive wines. There are now only a few people in the world who can afford to drink best quality French wines. Most bottles are bought as an investment and kept unopened in bank vaults. (What does it taste like when it's opened?)

Treading grapes by foot is making a comeback. Dirty feet are okay, it's soap residues that upset winemakers. No problems for them in France then.

As these elaborate laws are largely French bureaucracy laid down (as all good wine is) after long liquid lunches and are either ignored or irrelevant to the average tippler, the newcomer can happily concentrate on the basic essentials:
a) Does it taste good?
b) Does it make me feel good?
c) How long can I keep feeling good before I fall over?

More Wine

1. Select grapes.

2. Crush.

3. Ferment.

4. Filter.

5. Bottle.

6. Sell at huge profit to the English.

Top grape Varieties

Whites: *Chardonnay (Burgundy & Champagne), Chenin blanc (Loire), Sémillon (Bordeaux), Gewürztraminer (Alsace).*

Reds: *Cabernet sauvignon (Bordeaux), Pinot noir (Burgundy), Merlot (Bordeaux).*

French wines are named after where they are grown (Chablis and Beaujolais are French towns), except for Alsace, which follows German practice, and the Bordeaux reds that the English call 'claret'. Safe choices are Bordeaux and Burgundy reds and whites, Rhône reds, and Alsace and Loire whites.

Most everyday table wines (*vin de table*) are grown in the Languedoc-Roussillon region, the biggest wine-producing area in the world.

Much of the mystique of wine, thrown up by generations of alcohol-addled wine bores, is that nothing tastes, looks or means quite what it appears to. In order to hold your own (drinking or conversation-wise) in wine bore circles you need to understand some of the ambiguities of wine-speak:

• Colour •

White: Usually pale yellow. Sometimes clear. Never white. Whitewash is white.
Red: From purple to ochre. Rarely red.
Rosé: Pale red.

• Taste •

Dry: Acidic. More often described as crisp, flinty, fresh, tangy, smooth, zesty, fruity, rich, nutty, floral, oaky, buttery, heavy, light etc, etc.
Sweet: Sweet. Due to fermentation being stopped before all the grape sugar has changed to alcohol, or liquid sugar being added later. Dry wine cannot be made sweet by adding sugar. Not when your guests are looking anyway.

Champagne: Hideously expensive sparkling wine drunk out of fluted glasses or showgirl's shoes. The favourite tipple of social climbers world-wide although this has more to do with its snob appeal than its taste. Pink champagne looks nicer. But isn't.

Sec: Very dry.
Demi-sec: Not quite so mouth-puckering.
Doux: Sweet.

Sparkling: Fizzy. However, wine is never described as 'fizzy'. Wine is always 'sparkling', even if it's fizzing in a thick bottle with the cork held down with wire as it's liable to explode.

Still: Not sparkling, though it may still move about.

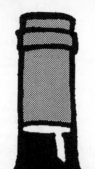

Even More Wine

Like food, the quality of wine improves the more of it that is consumed and the more it is talked about. You don't have to be an oenophile (wine expert), as in wine bore gatherings a lot of waffle goes a long way. Just stick to metaphors and indefinable subjects, such as smell or taste, and you will not go far wrong. Bear in mind that the tongue detects only four basic flavours: sweet, sour, salt and bitter; and above all, never ever comment on the quantity of the wine.

Smell: According to wine bores it has none. They refer to the smell of wine as 'aroma', 'bouquet' or most bizarrely, 'nose'. Strong smells are 'forward on the nose' and no smells 'behind the nose'. Presumably, if they sniff too close it's actually 'in the nose'.

Wine bores will say wine smells of almost anything: flowers, earth, wood, apples, petrol, even manure. Smells to do with their own interests are always worth an airing. Mention saddles, animals, farmyards, underwear, leather, jockstraps or money and you're well on your way to becoming accepted as one of them. Say it in French and you'll be given an oenophilic medal.

Tasty Terms

Beefy
Earthy
Firm
Forward
Fragrant
Hard
Long
Meaty
Penetrating
Robust
Silky
Smooth
Soft
Steely
Zesty

Connection with another pleasurable human activity is not coincidental

Taste: As taste is actually mostly smell, you can get away with substituting 'It tastes like...' for 'It smells like...'. However, you're not going to win any medals for 'It tastes like manure' (even if it does). Safer to employ the Classic French Shrug and stick to *bon, très bon,* and if you're really impressed: *très très bon!*

● Drinking red wine reduces heart disease, peps up sex lives and improves eyesight. It is also painfully evident in France that excessive consumption ruins livers and destroys brains.

Wine tasting: To assess by taste whether the liquid in your mouth has been passed through a donkey. Most people (except the English) can manage it. Wine bores, dedicated as always to making the simple complicated, indulge in a more elaborate ritual:

1. Pour
Have a vineyard worker pour a glass

2. Glare
To assess colour and clarity

3. Twirl
To release the bouquet

4. Slurp
Suck in air noisily with wine

5. Swill
To increase the tension

6. Express
Pass opinion

Serving: White wine (like wine bores) should be served 'lightly chilled' – an hour in the fridge or twelve minutes in the freezer, or if you forget served as an interesting iced lollipop to be passed round your guests.

Red wine should be served at room temperature and after it has been allowed to 'breath' (stand with the cork out). You may also 'decant', the simple act of pouring wine from a bottle into another container to separate the sediment, which wine bores turn into a semi-religious ritual involving a candle flame and cork sniffing.

White   Red   Champers   Brandy   Winelist

Glasses: Yes. Drinking from the bottle can ruin both your reputation and your best silk shirt.

Slurp!

What the label tells you: Not a lot, but they look as though they do. Some of them are also very pretty.

Bottled where grown.

The producer. Think of a name.

Picture of chateau. Often fanciful.

Capacity of bottle. Probably true. Though it's no guarantee that what fills it is all that is described on the label. In some regions another variety, vintage or source can be legally mixed in without mentioning it on the label.

The vintage. Date of grape harvest. Could be approximate.

If the label is in ***English***, French practice is to pour the wine down the drain immediately.

Grape variety. There are over 4,000. So what's different?

Appellation contrôlée. From a particular area. This bottle is the same as all the others.

Country of origin. The initials EU indicates wine dredged from a European wine lake.

NB: Relabelling is often not illegal.

Buying: Wine merchants have huge snob appeal and they will deliver in bulk. Most French drinkers buy at supermarkets – it's easiest. You can also buy direct from the producers. Take your own plastic jerricans (for wine not petrol, though some cars will run on cheap wine) and drink or bottle wine within a few months. Free tasting at a vineyard is a good excuse to try a few *crus*. Just don't expect to leave without buying something.

Wining and dining: The French drink wine with any meal and often with every meal (even breakfast). Indeed they consider 'a meal without wine is like a day without sunshine'. Most French people aren't wine snobs and will happily drink house wine in a restaurant and a full-bodied red with fish.

However, particular wines do complement certain foods. As a general rule, the stronger the food the stronger the wine; heavy reds with game and light whites with fish. Of course if the food tastes like old socks you won't find any drink (except cola perhaps) to go with it. If that happens (unlikely in France), leave the food and just drink. Wine is often included in fixed-price menus so you can drink as much as you like (within reason).

If you find pieces of cork in your wine do not scream: "CORKED!" and demand a replacement bottle. Cork doesn't harm wine. They are in close contact all the time. Just quietly spoon the pieces out. 'Corked' actually means that the cork has leaked air and turned the wine into something that tastes like rancid vinegar. A different thing altogether. It's an easy mistake to make but one which would label you an oenological ignoramus and ruin the meal for everybody.

● As most of a restaurant's profit comes from the sale of wine you will pay through the nose (or if you're a wine bore, through your 'bouquet') for the privilege of drinking it with your food. But don't try the miserly English trick of taking supermarket wine in with you. The French consider it deplorable bad taste. And it robs them of their huge profit.

Literature

The basic requirement of the great French novel is that it must always be about France. It must also be very long, deal with nature, the working class or elegant depravity and have no plot at all. Most of all the book must be impenetrable by the English. The fact that most French people cannot understand the original book in their own language isn't considered relevant. Like all French art, the novel does not exist to be understood but to be talked and argued about.

The newcomer to France will have enough to cope with without also trying to understand the labyrinthine complexities of French literature. Enough to acknowledge that these writers actually lived. To have knowledge of what they actually wrote about will elevate you to intellectual level in the eyes of the French.

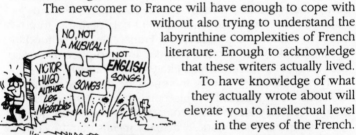

● French poetry, which takes nature, love and philosophy as its inspiration, is totally impenetrable and is best acknowledged with a shrug and a generous, 'C'est magnifique!'

· FRENCH NOVELISTS ·

Voltaire (1694-1778) Liberal, humanitarian and jailbird.
Jean-Jacques Rousseau (1712-78) Nature Romanticist.
Honoré de Balzac (1799-1850) Contemporary society.
Alexandre Dumas (1802-70) *The Three Musketeers*.
Victor Hugo (1802-85) Parisian epics. *Les Misérables*.
George Sand (1804-76) Womens' rights.
Gustave Flaubert (1821-80) Provincial bourgeoisie.
Emile Zola (1840-1902) Long-winded, lower-class life.
Marcel Proust (1871-1922) Boyhood and high society.
Colette (1873-1954) Titillation and childhood.
Jean-Paul Sartre (1905-80) Existentialist and Marxist.

Music

France has five million amateur musicians, over 300 music festivals, a government minister for rock and a worldwide reputation as the spiritual homeland of the musical tin ear.

But typically the French have turned their tone-deafness into an art form. Jazz is hugely popular, especially performed in smoky cellar clubs, the traditional lair of the intellectual beatnik generation. *Chanson française*, folk music for conveying ideas and information to the illiterate masses, also thrives in this pseudo-cerebral environment. French songs generally are always a triumph of lyrics over music.

To be a successful French singer you need a tremendous vibrato, a huge sense of the dramatic, and if possible die on stage. Good teeth and a heroic rise from the gutter are also useful attributes. Sacha Distel is the archetypal romantic French crooner, while tragedy pervades the voices of Charles Aznavour and the late Edith Piaf.

FRENCH MUSICIANS TO REMEMBER
Hector Berlioz (1802-69)
Founder of modern orchestration.
Georges Bizet (1838-75) Composer of the operas Carmen and The Pearl Fishers.
Claude Debussy (1862-1918) & *Maurice Ravel* (1875-1937) Musical impressionists.
Olivier Messiaen (1908-92) & *Pierre Boulez* (1925-) Modern radical composers.
Jazz violinist *Stéfane Grappelli* (1908-97) and the legendary three-fingered Gypsy guitarist *Django Reinhart* (1910-1953).

● French pop music is magnificently awful and unoriginal. Even the imitators are bad. Johnny Hallyday, the 1960s rock star who never had a hit outside France, still swivels his hips to great acclaim with the worst of them.

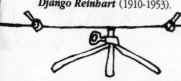

Film

The French make an art form of everyday life and turn everyday life into cinema. On screen, boring people become interesting and ordinary situations extraordinary. Even smoking can look quaintly attractive. The Hollywood slam-bang, kick-ass man blockbuster line has no place in the French director's manual. French cinema is introspection rather than demolition.

A tax on cinema tickets largely finances the industry. Paris has over 300 cinemas, most of them packed all day. And not always by sleeping tramps. Many show old films or reruns of classics, and stage seasons and festivals featuring a particular actor, director or theme.

Foreign films are shown with subtitles. Dubbed films are labelled VF (*version français*). Obscure but critically acclaimed films will be shown in their original language, VO (*version originale*). VA (*version anglais)* denotes an English-language film made acceptable by having a French-speaking director.

Foreign film titles translated into French often bear little resemblance to the original. Hollywood block-busters are considered virtual porn but the French still queue to watch them in droves. With their scarves pulled up and their berets pulled well down.

The Lumière brothers devised the first public cinema performance in 1895, then went on to make newsreel and documentary films. During the innovative 1920s and 30s, fantasy, pessimism, violence, poverty and social satire were all filmed for French screen entertainment.

The industry stagnated until the 1950s, when the new wave of directors including François Truffaut, Jean-Luc Godard and Louis Malle made films to please themselves rather than the studios (or the public). Roger Vadim brought Brigitte Bardot's sex-kitten sensuality to a panting world, but by the mid 1970s the new wave had run out of ideas.

Modern French cinema is considered elitist, boring and as unfathomable as the people themselves. Film story lines have been summed up as, 'Husband sleeps with Jeane because Bernadette upset him by sleeping with Christopher, and in the end they all go off to a restaurant.'

Gérard Depardieu is the best known French actor and a folk hero in his own country. Despite a huge nose and a waistline to match, women find him irresistible. When he turned down a big money film offer because it would interfere with his grape harvest, his popularity with the priority-conscious French soared to new heights.

Apart from introspection and unhappy endings, the French also like gentle, human comedy. Jacques Tati made comic films in the 1950s and 60s, featuring the bumbling Monsieur Hulot trying to adapt to an alien modern world.

French theatre's three biggest playwrights, Racine, Molière and Corneille, all lived in the 17th century. Beaumarchais wrote the operas *Barber of Seville* and *Figaro* in the 18th century. Irish-born Samuel Beckett introduced the 'theatre of the absurd' in the 1940s. Since then French theatre has become as impenetrable as French film.

Art

French museums and galleries are so full of art it overflows onto the streets and into the lives of ordinary people. Art is French life. French life is art.

However, newcomers are frequently shocked, surprised, mystified and angered by what passes for art in France. A glass pyramid blocking the entrance to the beautiful rococo-style palace, the Louvre. The oldest bridge in Paris wrapped in hundreds of yards of buff silk. A white-faced clown carrying a non-existent pane of glass across a square in a non-existent gale force wind. It's all art in France. If you feel moved to art criticism and actually kick the clown in an actual sensitive area you should claim in court that your action was actually Performance Art. You'll probably get away with it. French art is never what you do. It's always why you do it that matters.

Architecture: Roman artifacts abound in Provence. In the north, sublime 13th century Gothic cathedrals compete for the narrowest aisle and highest ceiling. The lavish ornate palaces of Fontainebleau and Versailles and the magnificent *châteaux* (castles) which litter the

Loire valley reflect all the pomposity, flamboyance and arrogance of the French monarchy.

Sculpture: At the end of the 19th century Auguste Rodin expressed romanticism in bronze and marble. His man and woman intimately entwined in 'the Kiss' and 'the Thinker' are both typically French themes of worldwide appeal and acclaim.

THE IMPRESSIONISTS

Camille Pissarro *(1830-1903)*
Free landscapes

Édouard Manet *(1832-83)*
Parisian middle class portraits

Edgar Degas *(1834-1917)*
Race courses and ballet

Paul Cézanne *(1839-1906)*
Still lifes, landscapes, cubism

Claude Monet *(1840-1926)*
Poppy fields, waterlilies

Auguste Renoir *(1841-1919)*
Figures in dappled shade. In later life voluminous nudes

THE POST-IMPRESSIONISTS

Paul Gauguin *(1848-1903)*
Exotic Tahitian women

Georges Seurat *(1859-91)*
Pointillism – unmixed paint dots

Henri de Toulouse-Lautrec *(1864-1901)*
Bars, brothels and music hall posters

Henri Matisse *(1869-1954)*
Fauvism – bright colours

Painting: Up to the 19th century the French Academy controlled conventions and kept painting in the European neo-classical tradition. Then the Paris-based Impressionists changed painting forever, exploring not merely the look of an object but also how the artist felt about it.

Manet experimented with composition and texture. Renoir, Monet and Pissarro with natural light. Monet kept painting the same subject in different light.

CLAUDE MONET
WATER LILIES
BY NIGHT

Pablo Picasso, though not French-born, did his best work in France. Dutch-born Vincent van Gogh worked in the south of France painting haunting self portraits and troubled landscapes. Impressionism led to a series of radical schisms: Pointillism, Cubism, Fauvism, Expressionism, Dadaism and Surrealism, but the second world war put an end to Paris as the world's artistic capital.

Culture 59

Fashion

The French love of fashion in all things becomes a veritable passion when it comes to clothes. They aren't just something to cover you up and soak up spilt wine (though they are to many French men); to the fashionable French, clothes are a statement of who they are and where they stand socially. The fact that many at the top of the clothes horse tree are sad fashion victims with more money than sense who stand next to anyone not dressed as expensively as they are at parties, does not stop fashion being a vital part of everyday French life. No self-respecting Parisienne would dream of being seen in public inappropriately dressed. Any woman in Paris not well turned out and chic will be a tourist.

The French fashion victim starts early. French children are usually immaculately dressed in designer clothes from an early age. American sports clothes, baseball hats and trainers are not part of the classical fashion scene, although teenagers in France are as badly dressed as they are in the rest of the world.

Fashionable French women dress in a simple, slightly formal style with lots of black. Sleek, well-cut hair and a flash of gold jewellery gives them the look and confidence of a defence lawyer about to destroy a dismally weak prosecution case.

Paris fashion houses fuel the French style ethos with ruthless creativity. Top of the range and hideously expensive is *haute couture*, one-off creations designed by couture houses listed with the *Fédération Française de la Couture*. (French bureaucracy even turns its heavy hand to making dresses).

Astronomical prices keeps *haute couture* exclusive (Dior flourishes with only a few hundred clients, many of them outside Europe) yet it remains the lifeblood and focus of the French fashion industry. Off-shoots are a highly lucrative business in *'prêt à porter'* (ready to wear) lines, perfumes, cosmetics and accessories.

Men don't usually have the luxury of *haute couture* dressing. Their choice is limited to ready-to-wear, but most of the big name women's wear designers also produce a range for men. Naturally, they too are hugely expensive.

Paris fashion shows are still vast media events and the designers as flamboyant, fey or reclusive as they ever were, but the rest of the world has caught up and Paris is no longer the fashion capital it was. However, when it comes to exclusivity, vanity and swagger the French are, as ever, in a class of their own.

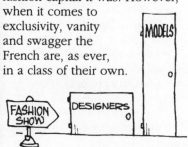

Top Designers

Coco Chanel:
The Little Black Dress. Chanel No. 5. Trench coats. Turtle neck sweaters. Jersey dresses. Bobbed hair.

Christian Dior:
1950s New Look.

Yves Saint Laurent:
Chic beatnik look. Trousers for women. Modern fashion shows of rock music and tall, skinny models.

Christian Lacroix:
1980s star with highly original and brightly coloured clothes.

Jean-Paul Gaultier:
Cone-shaped bra for Madonna. Skirts for men. Tattoos and body piercing.

● You are what you wear in a French city. A haversack will mark you out as a tourist, a shellsuit as American and football kit as an English hooligan. Union Jack shorts are below contempt everywhere.

French icons

Some French people and objects have about them a particular (or peculiar) quality of 'Frenchness' which make them impossible to imagine coming from any other country. Many are covered elsewhere this book, but there's a few more worthy of special attention:

Breasts: The French didn't invent them but they did most to thrust them into public scrutiny through extensive film and beach exposure. French breasts are small but being French are, of course, perfectly formed.

Descartes (1596-1650): Philosopher, stated the obvious – 'I think therefore I am.' But it wasn't obvious until he said it.

The baguette: Delicious when still warm from the oven. So is most bread when washed down with copious amounts of red wine.

Marcel Marceau: Mime artist who spawned an army of unspeakably tedious imitators.

Lumière brothers: Invented the film projector and the first cinema film. Nobody understood it but all said it was Great Art.

Napoleon: A man who liked to put one hand inside his waistcoat. What his hand was doing while in there is anybody's guess.

Brigitte Bardot: The original 'sex-kitten' film star. After a torrid personal life she declared she preferred animals to people. Then, as if to prove her point, she married an extreme right-wing politician.

The accordion: The only wind instrument capable of piercing the clamour of conversation in French restaurants.

First hot air balloon flight: (1783) Passengers were a duck, a sheep and a cockerel. Naturally they were all eaten at the celebratory dinner afterwards.

The can-can: One of the few dances (Zorba's is another) which can be done to only one tune.

Louis Blériot: First person to fly across the English Channel (1909). Thankfully without the Beaujolais Nouveau.

Pissoirs: Aromatic street urinals, largely replaced by scary high-tech superloos which disinfect themselves all over after each customer has (hopefully) left.

The sexy French maid: Good at turning down beds and much else.

Oh, là-là!: Mythical phrase devised to identify French characters (usually sexy chambermaids or waitresses) in English-speaking films and plays.

The onion seller: Combines three French passions; cycling, smelly food and taking money off the English.

Jacques Cousteau: Famous for making films underwater. Fortunately he first invented the aqualung.

Quasimodo: Fictitious but best known bell-ringer at Notre Dame cathedral.

Louis Pasteur: Discovered that germs cause illness. The suppository was invented soon after.

Business

French business is formal and so discreet as to be almost invisible. Visitors may even be so bold as to question whether it goes on at all. The French make work look like a hobby, a sideline to the main purpose of living: enjoying life.

Time-keeping is also treated as a triviality. French business people are routinely late for appointments. But as a minimum tolerance of half an hour is programmed into their genetic body clock, in their own eyes they are never late.

They have also never quite made up their minds about decision making. Discussions invariably move off at unpredictable tangents and talk switches to a new irrelevant subject with enthusiasm, but without any decision being reached on that either. Objectivity in business is distained as bureaucratic stifling of creativity.

However, managers and executives are decisive and efficient enough to avoid having to take work home and they never work at weekends. The traditional two-hour lunch break still hangs on, although executives often work (or so they claim to their partners) late in the evenings.

Despite periodic flirtations with socialism and a deeply held conviction of the power of the people, French workers are not keen on trade unions. They dislike joining formal organisations of any kind. But as French industry runs like French life, with everyone involved, they should have no complaints. This doesn't, of course, stop them complaining.

● Don't be misled by an apparent lack of urgency and the casual approach to business. They invariably mask ruthless and hard-headed business brains.

Bureaucracy

France is one of the world's most bureaucratic countries, with almost twice as many civil servants as Germany and three times as many as Japan. But however large the army of legislators it can never regulate people who don't want to be regulated. As de Gaulle said, 'It's difficult to rule a nation that has 365 cheeses' (or possibly 265, 400 or even 750). It's even harder to rule a country that has no idea how many cheeses it has.

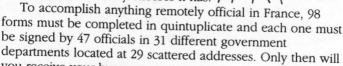

To accomplish anything remotely official in France, 98 forms must be completed in quintuplicate and each one must be signed by 47 officials in 31 different government departments located at 29 scattered addresses. Only then will you receive your bus pass.

The French attitude to petty regulations is to ignore them and they'll go away. Official communiques are routinely placed at the bottom of a large pile and forgotten. By the time officialdom decides to chase up the uncompleted form the rules will have changed and a new one will be required. This too goes to the bottom of the pile and the endless loop of bureaucratic form-filling creaks round another zillimetre.

What constitutes a 'petty' regulation and can thus be ignored has yet to be precisely defined by any regulatory body. It's not needed anyway, (though that doesn't usually stop the rulemakers) as the French consider all rules to be petty (unless they apply to somebody else).

● When dealing with officials never show impatience. Impatience is governed by a legislative body. Before you can show it to any official you must first complete the appropriate application forms.

Jobs

The French are traditionally farmers, but that role has been largely superseded and France has become a nation of restaurant, bistro and wine bar owners. In 1850, some 65% of the population worked on the land. That figure has now fallen to around 4%. The remaining one million agricultural workers keep busy by protesting on city streets at the merest hint of a reduction in EU farming subsidies.

French people like making things and not all of them come in bottles or on dinner plates. Their car industry is the fourth largest in the world. Motorways are being constantly built on which to race their cars and for the famously tetchy and militant French lorry drivers to regularly block with parked trucks and bring chaos to most of Europe. Heavy industry is still big in France, producing electric generators, turbines and transformers to power the world.

French warmongering hasn't gone out of fashion either.

Their aerospace industry employs more than 100,000 people making Mirage jets and Exocet missiles. France is the world's third largest exporter of armaments, after the old Soviet Union and the USA. The French arms sector alone employs some 300,000 people.

And, making itself even more unpopular, France is also the world's second biggest producer of nuclear power, with 55 stations on line and more under construction.

More positively, French flair (and British inventiveness) put Concorde on

the trans-Atlantic airways and the European Ariane unmanned rocket into space. French fascination with anything new has also nurtured a vibrant and prosperous computer and information technology industry.

Nevertheless, as unemployment usually hovers around 12% of the workforce, some 2.5 million people are permanently out of a job. Any newcomer looking for work must have something that a French person hasn't, which is difficult in a nation that has everything. Also as most jobs in France involve constant talk and argument, you must also be able to speak fluent and colloquial French.

To work legally requires a residence permit known as a *carte de séjour,* or if you live outside the EU another type of work permit, an *autorisation de travail.* This is difficult to obtain as your prospective employer must convince the authorities that there is nobody amongst the 2.5 million French unemployed who could do the job instead of you.

Work outside the law is fairly easy to find, but you will have no health, safety or minimum wage protection. It used to be called slavery.

● Some job opportunities in France:

Au pair (French for dogsbody): Childcare and housework. Somewhere to live plus pocket money.

Grape picking: Two weeks whenever grapes are ripe (unpredictable). Food and accommodation (unpredictable). Hardwork and low wages (predictable).

Fruit and vegetable picking: Five months work in various locations. Conditions much like grape picking.

Ski resorts: Cold, hard work, low wages and everybody else is on holiday.

Beach tourism: Hot, hard work, low wages and everybody else is on holiday.

Shopping

French shopping is among the best in the world. Seduced by the huge variety of shops, the stylish presentation and the high quality of goods on sale, it's

fatally easy to shop until you drop. Paris is THE shopping centre, world famous for its perfumes, jewellery, designer clothes, handbags, silk scarves and other fashion items.

France has the largest supermarkets outside America. Many towns boast a hypermarket, which is officially defined as a supermarket with over 2,500 square metres of floor space. By coincidence, that's about the same area as the deck space on a cross-Channel ferry loaded with British shopaholics desperate to spend their money on a fix. Hypermarkets are similar to department stores and sell a huge variety of goods in addition to food and drink.

French people shop in supermarkets and hypermarkets for convenience, but prefer the

Boulangerie: Baker's shop. Bread, croissants, small cakes and biscuits.
Confiserie: High class confectioner or sweet shop. Avoid if you're slimming.
Pâtisserie: Cake shop. Home-made pastries, fruit tarts and chocolate éclairs. All too beautiful to eat. (Force yourself!)
Crémerie: A dairy. Butter, cream, cheeses, eggs, yoghurt and ice cream, but usually doesn't sell fresh milk.

multitude of specialist shops for old-fashioned personal service (and local gossip). Some specialist shops are VERY specialised. Butchers sell either red meat, horse meat, pig meat or poultry, but rarely in the same shop. Collecting the ingredients for a mixed grill can take all day.

French bread is justifiably famous. Thanks to a 19th century law, all towns and villages above a certain size must have some kind of an outlet selling bread. The government controls price and weight, but not quality. Best eaten fresh and still warm, French bread goes stale quickly so bakers bake twice or even three times a day. It comes in a variety of shapes, sizes and ingredients. The *baguette* is the best known, the *pain* thickest and widest, while the *ficelle* is literally as 'thin as a piece of string'. Special ingredients can include raisins, nuts or even (gasp) chocolate!

French markets also thrive and are an experience not to be missed, even if you don't plan to buy anything. Amongst many other things, they sell fresh food and vegetables, and (sensitive souls should look away here) live animals and birds for the cooking pot. Stall-holders expect you to (gently) handle their goods and the livestock (very gently!). Ask to taste the cheeses, but you can help yourself to other displayed samples, usually olives or bon-bons.

FOOD SHOPS

Charcuterie: Delicatessen or pork butcher's shop. Cooked meats, quiches, omelettes, pizzas, salads etc.

Boucherie: Butcher's shop. All kinds of meat except horsemeat and often not pork either. May also sell poultry.

Boucherie chevaline: Horse butcher's.

Poissonnerie: Fish shop. Huge variety on offer. French fishermen never throw anything back.

More Shopping

French flea markets and antique markets are fascinating places to wander around. Apart from the obvious (but unlikely) possibility of picking up a priceless artefact for a few francs, there's also the added attraction of seeing what French people have in (or more correctly, have thrown out of) their houses. To most foreigners the interiors of French homes will always be a rarely glimpsed and mysterious world.

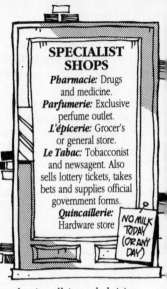

SPECIALIST SHOPS

Pharmacie: Drugs and medicine.
Parfumerie: Exclusive perfume outlet.
L'épicerie: Grocer's or general store.
Le Tabac: Tobacconist and newsagent. Also sells lottery tickets, takes bets and supplies official government forms.
Quincaillerie: Hardware store

NO MILK TODAY (OR ANY DAY)

Another puzzle for outsiders is the French distaste for fresh milk. Many supermarkets don't sell it and dairies treat it as something they shouldn't get involved with. Even more puzzling, given their renowned palate for food and drink, is the French preference for UHT long life milk, the dubiously-tasted concoction that was once fresh milk until the chemists got at it.

French teabags seem to have been similarly degenerated. They have the unusual ability to turn perfectly good water into something that even the slackest of public health authorities would condemn as being unfit for human consumption. No wonder the French prefer wine at tea time.

DEAR BUYS

Electronic and audio equipment, cameras, cosmetics, furniture, books and almost anything that's imported from outside the EU.

Beware also of fake goods. Some 70% of all fake products are copies of French brands. Perfumes are a favourite target, UHT milk and French tea bags are not (the originals are bad enough as they are).

WARNING

French clothes and footware are sized differently from other parts of the world. Don't buy anything without trying it on first.

Bargains are difficult to find in France. If you are offered one that seems too good to be true, it probably is.

However, if you see a queue outside a shop, join it. French shops are restricted to having a sale only twice a year so one is probably about to start. Of course they may just be queuing to buy the latest novelty: fresh milk.

Visitors to France should shop around and compare prices in France with those in their own countries. Having to constantly convert native currency into francs used to be enough for most people's mental arithmatic to cope with, but since 1999 the added complication of the euro has had to be brought into those increasingly complicated equations. 'Shop until you drop' has become 'shop until the value of your currency drops against the euro'.

Now for some good news. If you live outside the EU (and many people would consider that exceedingly good news), you're entitled to a refund of the value added tax on major purchases. Ask for the information on VAT – it's called TVA in France – before making a purchase.

● Don't get upset if the store staff are surly and unhelpful. They have to act like that. If they display a sunny and agreeable nature they could end up working at Euro Disney.

BEST BUYS

Quality clothes (including children's), fashion accessories, luxury goods, perfumes, decorative glass, kitchenware, domestic electrical equipment, toys, wines, liquors, and handicrafts.

Sport

Always a nation of rabid individuals, the French only play team games if it will help them conquer the world.

Rugby: Watched and played with passion. It offers the opportunity to knock hell out of the English in an international match without the bureaucratic niceties of declaring war or facing the indignity of being sunk by a gunboat in the English Channel.

Boules (also known in a less formal guise as ***pétanque***): A variation of the English game of bowls played with metal balls rather than woods. Despite an appearance as a demo sport in the 1992 Olympics, *boules* is more a pastime played by village men in work clothes, usually with a glass of *pastis* to hand. It looks sedentary but *boules* rouses so much passion it has to be controlled by a 70-page rule book.

Squash and tennis: Very popular. Both games are played by individuals and all French people look good in white.

Golf: France's fastest growing sport. Bolstered by tourist demand, courses are being built with a fervour previously reserved for building toll roads.

Cycling: Revered in France. Cyclists are the only thing French drivers will slow down for. The Tour de France is the world's biggest annual sporting event, watched by 20 million people along the route. Held in early summer, the race covers 2,500 miles in 21 daily stages, occasionally straying into neighbouring countries, which have to pay for the privilege. It's essentially French: colourful, pointless and it baffles the rest of the world. The French also like it because they can watch the race whizz by in seconds then spend the rest of the three weeks drinking and arguing about the results as they come in on TV.

Football: The national sport with over seven million players. Many top professionals play abroad showing off their style, panache and dazzling individual skills (they hate to part with the ball). To everyone's surprise (including their own) France won the World Cup in 1998, which triggered a huge outburst of ultra-patriotic rejoicing (no surprise to anybody).

Fishing: Enjoyed regularly by 20% of the population along the long coastline and in a multitude of lakes, rivers, streams and ponds. And the victor gets to eat the vanquished.

Hunting: France has two million registered hunters. You don't need a licence for a shotgun and they can be bought over the counter in hypermarkets. The French are notoriously bad shots and shoot themselves as frequently as they do the game. To get a hunting licence visitors must sit an exam in French, which keeps them out of the sport (and alive).

Bullfighting: *Corrida*, the Spanish-style of bullfighting where the bull is killed, is popular in the Basque country. In the Camargue pantomime version, white-clad *razeteurs* 'simply' remove ribbons tied to the bull's horns with hooks held between their fingers.

Outdoor sports: Unrivalled natural facilities and good weather for skiing, climbing, hiking, horse-riding, canoeing, swimming, sailing etc. And, as befits pioneers in aviation,

they still like to put their trust in air currents: ballooning, gliding, hang-gliding and paragliding.

● Before you take part in any kind of sport you must look the part and be kitted out in the latest fashionable gear. Looking a star is as important as winning. If you come last you can at least do it in style.

Cars

French cars were once the envy of the world; stylish, sexy and they weren't American. Now they are more utilitarian; simply

The Citroën Traction Avant

vehicles for getting about as quickly as possible (that's VERY quick) and humiliating and threatening fellow road users.

In French cities, particularly Paris where traffic moves at about the same speed as it did a hundred years ago, a car is an expensive liability, while in rural areas where public transport is almost non-existent, it's an expensive necessity.

There's little value in a French second-hand car. It will probably never have been cleaned inside or out and will bear the scars of a thousand 'coming togethers' on the motoring battlefields of France. The clutch will slip even though it has been replaced on a regular monthly basis, but the brakes will be in pristine condition. French drivers only use their car brakes if the horn doesn't work.

The French car industry is about a century old and is the fourth largest in the world after Japan, the USA and what used to be West Germany. More than half its production is exported. The industry employs 300,000 workers who produce almost four million vehicles (cars, vans and utility) a year. The two principal firms are the government-owned Renault, and Peugeot-Citroën (PSA) which is private. All three companies were founded before the first world war.

Citroën was founded by André Citroën who rarely drove a car and had no interest in motor sport. The Citroën

Traction Avant remains a much admired design icon whose sleek unique lines, made famous by the *Inspector Maigret* television series, evokes everything great about Thirties French cool. It was launched in 1934, the first front-wheel drive car in mass production and one that set the pattern for modern saloons. One Citroën model was called a 'Goddess'. Only the French could get away with naming a car 'goddess'.

The most famous French car is the much loved and much reviled 2CV, actually the Citröen Deux-Chevaux, powered by a two cylinder, six horsepower engine, which would be about right for a clockwork mouse. However, much of its appeal was the relative ease with which the least mechanically minded person could

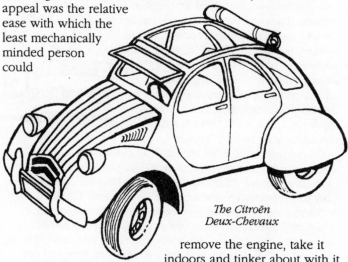

The Citroën Deux-Chevaux

remove the engine, take it indoors and tinker about with it on the kitchen table.

French cars have now largely lost their distinctive and eccentric appeal and have become just another part of the world market. Parts are now made in far flung countries where labour is cheap and the vehicles assembled in the

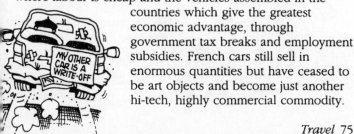

countries which give the greatest economic advantage, through government tax breaks and employment subsidies. French cars still sell in enormous quantities but have ceased to be art objects and become just another hi-tech, highly commercial commodity.

Driving

French people change character the moment they take control of a car. Normally aggressive, impatient and intolerant, they become aggressive, impatient and intolerant homicidal maniacs with an unshakable conviction in their own immortality the moment they turn the ignition switch of any motorised vehicle. They are theoretically capable of driving well as they must pass rigorous written and practical tests to qualify for a licence. However, once they've discarded their 'A' (for apprentice – and anarchist) plates most French drivers press their accelerator foot to the floor and keep it there for the rest of their lives.

Sometimes their lives are tragically short. Around 10,000 drivers are killed each year and 200,000 seriously injured – twice the number killed and injured in Britain, Japan or the USA in proportion to the number of vehicles. There's a road accident ever 5 seconds in France. When you drive there your life is literally in your (or more likely their) hands.

French law requires you to drive on the left hand side of the road. In practice (and they're always practicing it) the French drive on BOTH sides of the road. And on pavements, through hedges, across fields, down steps and up lampposts if necessary. French truck drivers believe they have a divine

right to all the road, all the time. They also have 40 tons of fast-moving hardware to back up their conviction. France has more than 3,728 miles of superb motorways.

The majority are toll roads and among the most expensive in Europe. But as French motorists (who can't pay or won't pay for motoring privileges) tend to keep off them they are safest roads in France.

Most main roads are designated priority roads; an admirable piece of legislation which purports to give vehicles on the main road priority over those coming onto it. Unfortunately, it's failed to register with French drivers who all assume they have sole priority over everything (except the skeletal figure in black with the scythe across his shoulder).

Interestingly, the French acquired their reputation for bad driving long before the motor car was invented. Travellers in the 18th century were terrified by the speed that horse-drawn carriages moved through the streets. The only changes the mighty internal combustion engine appears to have brought is to slow the traffic flow and increase the amount of tyre rubber left behind on the road at traffic lights.

Should you want to prove yourself equal to the French driving challenge (and if you do, you're on the wrong medication), try Paris on the first Saturday in August when the Parisians escape for their *grandes vacances*. If you survive that, you can do it all over again on the last Saturday of August when they return.

PIERRE'S CAR BODY REPAIR SHOP · PARIS ·

MY OTHER CAR IS A ROLLS ROYCE

Traffic lights

The sequence of red, green, yellow and red is generally interpreted by French drivers as go, go, go and go, but there are some subtleties:

 Red: Stop. However, in many cities there's a two-second delay after one set of lights changes to red and the other set changes to green. This is precisely the time it takes to cross a junction (or into the next life) with the accelerator pedal pressed hard to the floor.

 Green: Go. But if the driver in front is foreign or too slow (they always are) go along the pavement.

 Yellow: Stop at the stop line. But yellow is also the colour of chickens.

Overtaking – French style

1. Mirror. *After miles of tail-gating the car in front, and approaching the brow of a hill or a blind bend, check that no one is daring to overtake you.*

2. Signal. *The driver of the car being overtaken must be humiliated, especially if the car carries a foreign registration plate.*

3. Manoeuvre. *A word of French derivation meaning to cut in sharply, causing the other driver to brake heavily.*

French roundabouts resemble Rugby scrums with everyone charging, bashing, and pushing everyone else. It's easy for a visitor to lose all sense of direction (and the will to live). Remember, traffic flows anti-clockwise and vehicles on the roundabout have priority. Once you're on a busy roundabout (you'll have to push your way in) don't leave it until you're sure which is your exit. Study the road signs as you're carried around and around by the traffic. You won't even have to do much steering. When you're sure of your exit gradually move out towards the roundabout perimeter, keeping well away from any vehicle bigger or more battered than your own. Eventually (and if you haven't first died of old age or ran out of petrol), you can peel off with all the panache of a Grand Prix driver heading for the pits.

If after a few miles – and after a lively discussion with the rest of the occupants of your car over the merits of French road maps – you decide you're on the wrong road, simply turn round, go back to the roundabout and do it all over again. However, if you want to remain in a settled domestic relationship you should perhaps reconsider your suicidal wish to drive on the French roads and take a train instead.

Driving a car in a French city is a considerable risk to life and limb, but getting around on foot can be just as alarming. Using a pedestrian crossing is the motoring equivalent of Russian roulette. Every vehicle could have your name on it but you don't know when the actual one is coming. The only certainty is that none of them will stop for anything as insignificant as a pedestrian crossing (or a pedestrian).

● Don't drive in bus, taxi or cycle lanes. Buses are bigger than you, taxi drivers are often part-time boxers or wrestlers and city cyclists are invariably lawyers with a nifty line in motoring litigation.

Public Transport

French towns and cities generally have excellent public transport. Elsewhere it varies between poor and non-existent. Miss a bus in the country and you could wait the rest of the year for the next one. Paris, the country's international shop window of how good it can do everything, has one of the most efficient, best integrated and cheapest public transport systems in the world. The world famous *métro*, an extensive suburban rail network and comprehensive bus services are all totally integrated with tickets that can be used on all three systems. Government subsidised, it's also inexpensive.

The French, who are habitually late for everything, expect punctuality in their public transport. A train two minutes late is enough to spark a passenger invasion of the driver's compartment to demand a satisfactory explanation.

Trains: France has the largest system in Europe, with more than 21,000 miles of track centred on Paris (to get anywhere you have to go via Paris). It's state-owned with SNFC as operator and carries some 800 million passengers a

year. Pride of the French rail system is the high speed TGV (*Train à Grand Vitesse*) which rockets along at speeds of up to 186mph between 50 French cities. On a rushed day it achieved 320mph, a world record. Sadly, the TGV also has to suffer the indignity of operating through the Channel Tunnel, where it has to slow down to snail pace as soon as it gets onto the antiquated and ramshackle British rail system.

Métro: A number of French cities have an underground railway. The fully automatic line in Lille operates without drivers (pity it can't be extended to the roads). The Paris *métro*, which dates from 1900, has some 123 miles of track and you're usually never more than 500 yards from a station. Some 4.5 million people use the *métro* daily.

Taxis: Paris has more than 15,000 taxis – ordinary cars with a meter and a light on top. They're often difficult to find, particularly during lunch times, rush hours, when it's raining or when there's a big sporting fixture on TV.

You also have to put up with the drivers. French taxi drivers go through a stringent screening system to ensure that only the most unscrupulous, rudest and unruly are allowed to miscarry the travelling public. You can only hail a taxi in the street if it's at least 50 yards from a taxi rank. Whether it stops depends on the mood of the driver.

Buses: Generally good services in the cities but in the country there's usually one bus in the morning and another at night to cater for the needs of schoolchildren, workers, and shoppers on market days. Even that service can dry up during school holidays. France has no national bus company operating on a countrywide basis.

Airline services: The state-owned national airline, Air France, and its domestic wing, Air Inter, have a virtual monopoly of French airspace. Consequently, they are amongst the world's most expensive. Business fares are the biggest rip-offs. However, flying is often cheaper and faster than the train on domestic routes. You can reach anywhere in France in an average time of one hour and with only a 30-minute check-in time. The internal routes are so short the in-flight drinks trolley goes round at the speed of a TGV.

Charles de Gaulle airport, France's showpiece, lies 23 miles north-east of the centre of Paris. Like its namesake, it's big, self-important and baffling. But unlike the late president, it doesn't like to say '*non*' or keep out the British. Especially when they've got fists full of francs to spend.

The Media

Since government control was abolished in 1974, French television has become a downmarket mixture of foreign programmes badly dubbed into French, moronic game shows and endless repeats of ancient favourites, many in black and white and featuring long-dead performers (television personalities never die in France, they just become repeats).

Circus, that peculiarly French passion for the bizarre, is  permanently shown on one channel or another. Soap operas roll endlessly on and a daily diet of chat shows ruthlessly exploit the French love of talking (but saying very little of substance). French television is trashy. It's inconsequential. And the French love it. Even the middle classes (who profess never to watch television as it insults their lofty intelligence) like it because it gives them something to look down on and moan about.

France has six national channels, each with varying amounts of advertising (often the most entertaining parts), and 60 satellite channels beaming programmes from seven different countries. Critics routinely attack the main television channel (TF1) for not making enough French programmes, but viewers want to watch trashyvision and it's cheaply available from all over the world. Oddly, satellite television hasn't caught on in France and is mainly watched by expatriates. It's probably too upmarket for the natives.

Television reception standards are different in France (so much is) so you will have to invest in a French-built receiver and video recorder before you can 'enjoy' the country's output. The SECAM system (the rest of the world's television runs on PAL or NTSC) was designed to keep French television French. Naturally, it's been a glorious failure.

Television reception varies considerably throughout France and in remote areas (outside Paris) it can be as poor as the programmes (unwatchable).

Radio: A mixture of public service broadcasting and private commercialism. Deregulation spawned scores of stations playing wall to wall British and American pop music. Horrified French purists forced through new regulations which ordered 40% of output to be French music. This led to many stations closing down, convinced that no audience would ever willingly listen for 40% of the time to the likes of Sasha Distel.

Phone-in programmes attract big audiences as the French are obsessed by all aspects of human behaviour. They like to listen while doing something else (talking probably), or driving to work (the callers are as angry as the drivers) and everyone joins in (whether they are on the phone or not).

Newspapers: The French generally prefer words to pictures and like to read opinions which are similar to their own. Among the numerous regional and national publications there's a newspaper for every political view.

The best known, *Le Monde* and *Le Figaro* are Paris based and not widely read nationally. Regional newspapers are just as important and match the big two in circulation figures.

The handful of English speaking papers are aimed at British and American expatriates and predictably reflect their priorities in France: jobs, accommodation and services.

● Listening to television and radio can help you to learn French and brush up your pronunciation. Careful though, you could end up sounding like a French game show host.

Post and Phone

French telecommunications are among the best in Europe and were the first to provide customers with a minitel service. This wondrous database furnishes all the facilities of the Yellow Pages, gives rail, bus and airline timetables, books theatre seats and probably phones home when you are held up, puts your dinner on a low heat and walks the dog also. What it doesn't supply is civility. Even French computers cannot manage civility.

Phone a stranger in France and you'll get the impression that you are interrupting some form of business far more important than what you are phoning about. French people generally don't like talking on the phone. It cramps their body language. The standard way of answering the phone is a brusque *'allô'* or if the recipient is feeling friendly or humourous (it does happen), *'allô, allô!'*

The postal service is fast, reliable, bureaucratic but expensive, especially when posting abroad. About three-quarters of domestic letters arrive the day after posting. The rest are treated to a world tour taking in Australia, the Arctic regions and the Amazon rain forest. French post offices provide a huge range of services but you must queue at the right window. Choose the wrong one and you will have to go to the end of another long queue at another window. It can take longer to post your parcel than it takes to deliver it.

The highly automatised postal system is generally efficient but it cannot eliminate the human element. French postal workers are all serial shredders. If you're sending anything remotely fragile make sure it's well packed. Assume it's going to be thrown from the Eiffel tower and dragged through rush hour Paris streets in a thunderstorm. Anything carrying British stamps probably will be.

Education

French education is acclaimed for its high academic standards and the excellent state-funded school system. It's free and compulsory until the age of sixteen, but children are expected to work seven-hour school days followed by extensive homework. They attend kindergarten from three to six years of age, primary school until eleven, then various systems of secondary education leading to the famous *baccalauréat* (higher school certificate). *Le bac* is the essential qualification in a country that loves qualifications. Parents will do anything (including bribery and corruption) to ensure that their children will succeed.

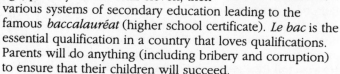

The country rates education top priority and devotes roughly 20% of the state budget to its students and teachers. Some 30% of young French people go on to further education, the highest proportion in Europe. France has more than 70 universities, 13 of them in Paris. Long queues, swelled by scrummaging parents, quickly form outside the most prestigious as soon as *le bac* results are announced.

The once iron grip of government on education has loosened and now schools are allowed to choose what they want to teach for 10% of curriculum time. Traditionalists are shocked by the decline in teaching of glorious French history and literature in favour of technology and science. But in 1998 the French education system was given a ringing endorsement that French youth has absorbed traditional ways of doing things when 30,000 secondary school pupils took to the streets to protest about school conditions. In the time-honoured manner the protest turned into a riot and pupils fought with the CRS riot police. The future of France is in safe hands. Hands that have learnt how to throw paving slabs.

Police Business

The French police have a reputation for being tough, vain, heavily corrupt and more tied up with fighting bureaucracy than crime. Crimes have to be pretty serious before they enter the police files. Murder, arson and fiddling the divisional *boules* league results just about make it.

Rural police follow a relaxed approach to crime and most would consider Hercule Poirot a radical hot head. If you report a crime they'll refer you to the gendarmerie in the next village, then return to their important investigation on the supply of truffles to the local restaurant. However, if they take a dislike to you, you can be thrown in the cells for up to 24 hours without being charged.

French law is an extension of real life (and we all know how chaotic that can be). The system is based on logic, argument, persuasion, arm-twisting and the exchange of large brown envelopes stuffed with money – an arbitrational rather than an adversarial model. One side is not wrong and the other side right. The object is to arrive at a version of the truth that all sides can agree on and who's going to pay for dinner afterwards.

POLICE FORCES

Police nationale:
Controlled by the Interior Ministry. Local crime.

Gendarmerie nationale:
Part of the army. Serious crime, road traffic, rescue.

Compagnie Républicaine de Sécurité (CRS):
Riot police. Extremely dangerous. Fearsome appearance modelled on comic book hero, Judge Dred.

● Address French policeman as *'monsieur l'agent'*. They are commonly know as *flics* (cops) and much, much worse. It's safer not knowing what. Never forget that all French police carry guns.

Military Matters

As befits a country graced with all manner of enviable riches but also burdened with an unenviable history of being invaded and occupied, France is hypersensitive about its national security.

Defence spending accounts for some 15% of the total state budget. Between the ages of 18 and 26 all male French nationals (anyone with one French parent), even ones that live abroad, are liable for compulsory military service for 10 months, 16 if they become officers. About a third of France's more than 600,000 servicemen are conscripts. After years of furious questioning (especially by males aged 18 to 26), French conscription is due to be abolished in line with most of Europe. One way to avoid national service is a certificate of insanity from a doctor. But as in the classic Catch-22 situation, to be in the French military you have to be crazy.

Ever since de Gaulle said 'non' to NATO in 1966, France has been independent (VERY independent) and relies on its own nuclear deterrent, tested in the South Pacific to the fury of the rest of the world. However, as always enjoying the best of both worlds, France has not altogether left the Atlantic Alliance and still takes part in NATO manoeuvres. It has also cunningly forged strong links with Germany, the old enemy and its biggest rival in western Europe for military might, through the joint France-German brigade.

The French have always been extremely proud of their army and the country has monuments all over the place to its war heroes and 'glorious' victories both ancient and modern.

Government

The French like government. It makes them feel someone cares (even if they don't). They see their government of whatever party as the embodiment of France itself, strutting the world power stage with the rest of the world tagging along out of step. Domestically, the main purpose of government is to expose scandals perpetrated by the one before it. With corruption as rampant as a French politician's sex life, they always have plenty to choose from.

Power in France is shared between president, government and parliament (the unholy trinity). The president heads the

executive and elects ministers to do the work while he (France has yet to be ruled by a woman – Margaret Thatcher, when British prime minister, came closest) concentrates on the important business of sneering at the rest of the world, banqueting at foreign expense and keeping a string of mistresses happy. He lives, appropriately, like a king in the Elysée palace.

Parliament consists of two chambers: the National Assembly and the Senate. Bills pass through both chambers. If they disagree (they usually do) a joint committee is set up to attempt to reach an amicable solution. If this fails (it usually does), the National Assembly has the final say. The next layer of long-winded (and hot-aired) government is the Constitutional Council which has to ensure that all laws passed are constitutional.

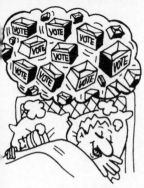

Elections are held more or less continuously and are decided by a unique form of proportional representation requiring two polls a week apart to give voters time to change their minds. This voting system invariably produces a coalition holding the balance of power, which leads to continual argument, back-stabbing and deals struck in smoke-filled rooms.

Even more tumult is generated by the president being elected every seven years and the National Assembly every five years, so there are inevitably times when the two bodies are out of step and represented by different (and hostile) political parties.

Membership of the EU brings yet more legislation, confusion and stalemate into which career politicians can weave their own powerful and profitable empires. France sees the EU as of great importance (nothing is more important than furthering your own interests).

On top of all this, local government provides a further fertile breeding ground for bureaucracy and empire building to proliferate. For administrative purposes, France is divided into 22 regions and 96 *départments*. Each *départment* has a general council and a government representative, and is subdivided in ever diminishing sizes into *arrondissements, cantons, communes,* mayors, villages, restaurants, waiters, tables, plates, snails, shells and so on. Each region also has an elected council and officials, but to avoid conflict with the *départment* level of the hierarchy they have limited power and play no part in actual administration.

France also owns overseas territories (many with ownership disputed by independence movements or other countries) whose administrations are so impenetrable the French government doesn't know how they are run, why they are French or even where the territories are.

Houses

Most French families live in detached homes or apartments; semi-detached and terraced properties are relatively rare. They aren't as house proud as some nationalities and tend to pay scant attention to the interior decoration of their homes and often neglect their gardens. Air conditioning is  surprisingly rare and (unsurprisingly) many older houses don't have a bath, shower room or an inside toilet.

As the French dislike commuting to work, there's been an exodus of people from the land to the cities and factories, leaving an estimated 13% of rural properties standing empty and prices plummeting. This offers foreigners the tempting opportunity to buy a size or style of home that they couldn't afford in their home country.

However, it's all too easy to fall in love with the beauty and ambience of France and buy a property without giving it sufficient thought. The French are often amazed by the prices that foreigners are prepared to pay for derelict properties that nobody else will touch (although they never complain). If you fancy lording it up in your own *château*, bear in mind that the reason so many of them are on the market at such reasonable prices is that the cost of restoration and upkeep is astronomical and you will probably have to make huge sacrifices back home to maintain your elevated status.

• CHATEAU•

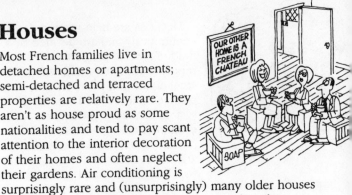

• FARMHOUSE•

Also remember that you're not simply buying a home but a lifestyle. Your best chance of being accepted by the French is to do as they do (it's usually the easiest way of doing things anyway). Importing aspects of your own culture which may upset the natives is asking for trouble.

The vast majority of house sales are through estate agents. France has a unique system of property purchase and conveyancing which the average foreign buyer may well consider cumbersome, expensive and unnecessarily legalistic. That's hardly surprising as it's strictly controlled by French law and can only be carried out by a *notaire* who represents neither the seller nor the buyer, but the French government. Don't expect a *notaire* to speak your language or to explain the intricacies of French law. For that you will need a solicitor (and a deep pocket).

Never be tempted by the 'quaint' French custom of tax evasion, where the 'official' sale price declared to the tax authorities is reduced by an under-the-table cash payment. This practice is strictly illegal (and widespread).

However, the process usually works well (eventually) and you can end up living your dream in rural France, savouring your *vin de pays* on your sunkissed patio and exchanging a friendly *'bonjour'* with your French neighbours. Only they won't be there. They've moved to the city.

• GITE •

• BARGAIN? •

Renovation

Any foreigner who sets out to renovate a derelict property in France must have courage, determination, money and an extensive vocabulary of French swear words to overcome the many problems, people and unimaginable provocations they will inevitably face. They must also be prepared to have their sanity repeatedly questioned by everyone (including themselves). It's useful to remember (preferably BEFORE buying one) that many 18th and 19th century farmhouses will have been almost totally neglected SINCE THEY WERE BUILT and that an empty property in a remote area is empty because nobody wants to live in it.

... AND WE'LL THROW IN A MACHETE AND A FLAME THROWER JUST TO GET YOU STARTED

However, the decision to renovate a property will bring you into close contact with the essence of living in France: getting anything done. Even getting the things to do anything with can be a problem. The French are not keen on do-it-yourself (it requires effort) so unless you settle near a DIY chainstore (who LOVE foreign DIY fanatics), materials are more difficult to find than in other countries. As you search, you will soon realise that the driving times to the nearest towns quoted at the buying stage of your property were achieved by a formula one racer in a hurry (or an average French driver).

A working knowledge of the French language is also essential, especially the accurate and exact words for particular items and measurements. Even then you will still be routinely delivered something completely different from what you ordered. Keep cool and regard it as a softening up process preparing you for the more relaxed French approach

to life. After all, isn't that why you want to live there anyway?

Never start any building work until you have official permission. This involves extensive and wide-ranging discussions with building workers (which will inevitably require some dexterity with a corkscrew) and extensive scrutiny of your plans by the mayor and the town council, who are very important and influential figures in local administration (especially when you want planning permission from them).

French workmen have in the past been criticised by a minority of foreign buyers (some foreigners have even made fortunes from books complaining about the workers) but most praise their quality of work and reasonable prices. Just don't expect anything to be finished on time.

When everything's completed and you've recovered from your 19th nervous breakdown, you can then profitably let your dream home to envious guests while you bask in the glory of owning a home in your favourite tourist area. Unfortunately, when you live there in the summer, you'll probably find the place overrun by intrusive foreign tourists. *Bienvenue en France!*

If you're *serious*
about France . . .

Buying a Home in France

Survival Books' 'Buying a Home' series is the most comprehensive and up-to-date source of practical information about buying a home abroad. Other books in this series include *Buying a Home Abroad*, plus *Buying a Home in Britain* (summer 1999), Florida, Ireland, Italy, Portugal and Spain. Survival Books are available from good bookshops throughout the world or direct from Survival Books.

Order your copies today by phone, fax, mail or e-mail from:
Survival Books, PO box 146, Wetherby, West Yorks. LS23 6XZ, United Kingdom.
Tel/fax: +44-1937-843523, e-mail: orders@survivalbooks.net,
Internet: www.survivalbooks.net.

We accept payment by credit/debit cards. If you aren't entirely satisfied simply return books within 14 days for a full and unconditional refund.

you need these two books . . .

Living and Working in France

Survival Books' 'Living and Working' series is the most comprehensive and up-to-date source of practical information about everyday life abroad. The other titles in this series include America, Australia, Britain, Canada (summer 1999), New Zealand, Spain and Switzerland. Survival Books are available from good bookshops throughout the world or direct from Survival Books.

Order your copies today by phone, fax, mail or e-mail from:

Survival Books, PO box 146, Wetherby, West Yorks. LS23 6XZ, United Kingdom.

Tel/fax: +44-1937-843523, e-mail: orders@survivalbooks.net,

Internet: www.survivalbooks.net.

We accept payment by credit/debit cards. If you aren't entirely satisfied simply return books within 14 days for a full and unconditional refund.

Order Form

Unit prices *

Qty	Title	UK	Europe	World	Total
	Alien's Guide to France	£6.95	£7.45	£8.45	
	Buying a Home Abroad	£11.45	£12.95	£14.95	
	Buying a Home in Britain (Sep 99)	£11.45	£12.95	£14.95	
	Buying a Home in Florida	£11.45	£12.95	£14.95	
	Buying a Home in France	£11.45	£12.95	£14.95	
	Buying a Home in Ireland	£11.45	£12.95	£14.95	
	Buying a Home in Italy	£11.45	£12.95	£14.95	
	Buying a Home in Portugal	£11.45	£12.95	£14.95	
	Buying a Home in Spain	£11.45	£12.95	£14.95	
	Living and Working in America	£14.95	£16.95	£20.45	
	Living and Working in Australia	£14.95	£16.95	£20.45	
	Living and Working in Britain	£14.95	£16.95	£20.45	
	Living and Working in Canada (Aug 99)	£14.95	£16.95	£20.45	
	Living and Working in France	£14.95	£16.95	£20.45	
	Living and Working in London (Oct 99)	£11.45	£12.95	£14.95	
	Living and Working in New Zealand	£14.95	£16.95	£20.45	
	Living and Working in Spain	£14.95	£16.95	£20.45	
	Living and Working in Switzerland	£14.95	£16.95	£20.45	
				TOTAL	

Cheque enclosed/ Please charge my Access/Delta/Mastercard/Switch/Visa* card.

Expiry date _ _ _ _ _ _ _ _ _ _ _ _ _ _ _ _ _ _ _ No. _ _ _ _ _ _ _ _ _ _ _ _ _ _ _ _ _ _

Issue number (Switch only) _ _ _ _ _ Signature _

*Delete as applicable (prices for Europe/World include airmail postage)

NAME _

ADDRESS _

_ _

Send to: Survival Books, PO Box 146, Wetherby, West Yorks. LS23 6XZ.
United Kingdom **or tel/fax credit card orders to +44-1937-843523.**